The Search for Faculty Power

University of Toronto Faculty Association

720 Spadina Avenue, Ste 419
Toronto, ON M5S 2T9
416.978.3351

February 14, 2007

Dear Colleague:

As a member of UTFA, please accept a complimentary copy of the 2006 updated reprint of Bill Nelson's 1993 book: _The Search for Faculty Power: The History of the University of Toronto Faculty Association._

When I became President of your Faculty Association, I turned to Bill's book as our institutional memory. It served me well. It provided information, insights, and judgements.

On the last page, the author writes:

> *"It certainly serves little purpose for the Faculty association and the University administration, each to question the legitimacy of the other. They are colleagues and they are adversaries. So it has been, and so, presumably, it will be."*

I hope you will read the book and that perhaps while doing so decide to become more engaged with UTFA.

Sincerely

George Luste
Physics Professor and
UTFA President
luste@utfa.org

The Search for Faculty Power

The University of Toronto Faculty Association
1942-1992

William H. Nelson

The University of Toronto Faculty Association
Canadian Scholars' Press
TORONTO, CANADA

Nelson, William H., 1923-.

The Search or Faculty Power: The University of Toronto
Faculty Association, 1942-1992

First published in 1993 by
**The University of Toronto Faculty Association
720 Spadina Ave., Suite 419
Toronto, M5S 1A1
Canada**
and
**Canadian Scholars' Press Inc.
180 Bloor Street West, Suite 402
Toronto, M5S 2V6
Canada**

Canadian Cataloguing in Publication Data

Main entry under title:

The Search for Faculty Power: The University of
Toronto Faculty Association, 1942-1992

ISBN 1-55130-023-0

1. University of Toronto Faculty Association - History. I.
Title.

LE3.T52N44   1993   378.1'2'09713541
C93-0940000-8

Contents

2006 Preface

It seems useful, in reprinting my book on the history of the Faculty Association, to add a brief summary of some of the main events and trends in the association over the fifteen years since I wrote the book.

It requires no insight to see that most of the defining events of faculty relations with the university have been driven, directly or indirectly, by concerns about security—security of tenure, of salary and benefits, of professional status and academic freedom. The early 1990s saw what seemed at the time a grave threat to all these aspects of faculty security. Along with an abatement of inflation, there was in Ontario especially an increasingly grim contraction of public spending on higher education relative to other public spending. The attempt to enforce a "social contract" by Bob Rae's NDP government was a direct attack on collective bargaining, and included threats to jobs, salaries, and pensions in the universities. At the University of Toronto the administration cut jobs sharply among some non-academic staff. Despite various threatening gestures, there were no actual cuts among tenured faculty, though there were in the teaching stream.

One particularly savage attempt at job-cutting occurred in the Faculty of Medicine in November 1991: disregarding established procedures for terminating jobs and, instead, following the advice of a private consultant, a personnel officer in the Faculty of Medicine persuaded the Dean of Medicine and the central administration in Simcoe Hall to carry out a sudden, unannounced firing of 79 employees in the faculty. People with many years of service were given hours or minutes to clear out of their offices, university police standing by to enforce expulsion. The whole body of university employees, academic and non-academic, was outraged. And, as had happened before in times of crisis, in the absence of any other institution, such as a faculty senate, the Faculty Association took the lead in resisting the firings. A well-attended and somewhat unruly general meeting passed motions demanding the reinstatement of the fired employees as well as an apology from University of Toronto President Robert Prichard. In the event, there were no formal apologies, the dismissed employees were reinstated, and this style of job termination was not repeated.

But the loss of non-teaching jobs, especially in the library, continued for years. And the university administration attempted to limit faculty benefits. In 1994-95 there was no across-the-board salary increase and no PTR. There were various threats to the progress-through-the-ranks component of salaries, which for twenty years had been the basis of faculty salary structures, and, as well, increasing rigour in awarding tenure, and increasing reliance on non-tenured staff for teaching. Though the worst fears were not realized, it was this climate of contraction, reduction, and menace that sent a chill through the university in the 1990s.

Fortunately, the mechanism for hearing grievances laid out in the Memorandum of Agreement did provide some protection for faculty members, and, not surprisingly, the number of formal faculty grievances burgeoned in the 1990s. Some 500 grievances were heard in the five years after 1996, before falling sharply in recent years from 100 a year to 20 or 30. Many of the grievances of the '90s concerned PTR awards, and the recent fall in numbers reflects both more uniform administrative procedures and a slightly milder benefits climate.

Of course, the great grievance issue in these years was centred on a grievor who was not a regular university faculty member at all. This was Nancy Olivieri, a doctor at the Hospital for Sick Children in Toronto, who was engaged in research concerning thalassemia and related blood disorders. Her research was being partly funded by a drug company, one of whose products Dr. Olivieri was testing on her patients. When the results of her research led her to conclude the drug in question was ineffective and possibly harmful, she published her conclusions and found herself under attack from the drug company and the hospital administration. Olivieri was fired as head of her research program and sued by Apotex, the drug company. She, along with several of her co-workers, appealed to UTFA for support.

The position of clinical staff in the hospitals who also hold university titles has never been entirely clear. UTFA does not negotiate their salary and benefits or represent their interests generally. They are rarely members of UTFA, though some have been over the years. But they do hold university titles—Olivieri was a full professor—and they have a common interest with regular university faculty in the freedom to do unhindered research and publish its results. The Faculty Association agreed to represent Olivieri, not anticipating that her appeal would go on for five years, from 1997 to 2002, and threaten to bankrupt the association.

The Olivieri case was complex and studded with extraneous issues. Faculty support for UTFA's representation of Olivieri was not unanimous, and weakened somewhat as the years drew on. It was argued that she and her co-grievors should seek the support of other clinicians in the hospitals rather than UTFA's (there was, and is, no effective negotiating body representing medical clinicians). Doubts were raised about Olivieri's research, and she was subjected to various forms of harassment, ranging from denial of hospital facilities to attacks on her and her colleagues in anonymous letters. The relationship between the university and the teaching hospitals was not straightforward. There were entangling complications, such as the university's expectation of a major donation from Apotex. A mediated settlement of the case reached early in 1999 fell apart after further hospital harassment of Olivieri and her supporters. With remorselessly rising legal expenses and dwindling funds, UTFA sought support from CAUT and received it unstintingly, including a $200,000 grant to apply to lawyers' bills.

As time went on, the Faculty Association came under pressure from some of its members to drop its support of Olivieri, or, perhaps, accept a cosmetic settlement that would amount to the same thing. But even as UTFA was feeling the strain of this case, so were the hospital and university administrations. The Olivieri appeal was drawing national and, indeed, international attention. It was increasingly viewed as a fundamental test of academic freedom in a world where corporate donations were replacing public funds in financing research. Toronto hospitals and the university disliked the bad publicity and feared the wrath of donors. CAUT's solid support made it clear that UTFA had resources beyond its own. Finally, in the fall of 2002, with the tough mediation of Martin Teplitsky, Olivieri and UTFA won a major victory. The terms of the settlement included an agreement on their confidentiality, but it was clear that the university and the Hospital for Sick Children had capitulated. A part of the settlement that could not be kept confidential was a $500,000 payment from the university to UTFA for legal expenses.

The Olivieri case was the most important test of academic freedom in Canada since the Crowe case in the 1950s. In that affair the Toronto Faculty Association had been timid, passive, and unhelpful. But UTFA passed the Olivieri test. It is to the credit of the three UTFA presidents who were involved in the Olivieri appeal—Bill Graham, Rhonda Love, and George Luste—that they, supported by the UTFA Executive and Council, kept their nerve and their principles.

In December 2002, a few weeks after the Olivieri settlement, University Provost Shirley Neumann, quite recently arrived at Toronto and perhaps not wholly familiar with its traditions, dropped a bombshell on UTFA by abruptly invoking Article 21 of the Memorandum of Agreement to give notice of the agreement's termination. The Provost explained that she only wanted, once and for all, to remove clinical faculty from any claim to UTFA's support, and had no way to do this except by terminating the agreement so as to make slight revisions in it. In a special meeting, the UTFA Council voted unanimously to consider certification. With advice and assistance from CAUT and some certified unions at other universities, UTFA started to organize a certification drive. For a few weeks it really seemed that the Toronto faculty would finally join most of the other universities of Canada in seeking full unionization. Early in February 2003, however, fortunately or unfortunately, the provost rescinded her notice of termination, and the wind quickly went out of the sails of certification.

For a number of years until 1992, the Faculty Association's own management and financial state appeared to be satisfactory. UTFA's annual revenue and expenditures had both risen to about a million dollars, and reserves had climbed to not much less than that. Then, however, the association began having money troubles. Reserves fell by half in three years. Office expenses, mainly staff salaries, had risen sharply, as had legal and other expenses associated with salary and benefit negotiations.

Suzie Scott, UTFA's Executive Director, had routinely made recommendations on staff salaries and other expenses to the UTFA Executive, and these had usually been approved without change. But in 1994 the new Treasurer, Andrew Oliver, challenged Scott's recommendations, and in 1995, Oliver, now Salary and Benefits Chair, continued his criticisms. Scott vigorously defended her proposals. Most of the executive supported Oliver, but a couple of members and the new president, Peter Boulton, supported Scott. While the president and executive attempted to find a solution, without making the dispute public, the council, angry at not being consulted, lost confidence in both Boulton and his executive. Boulton had been acclaimed for a second term, but decided to resign at the end of his first year. A summer election was held with two former presidents as candidates: Fred Wilson, perceived as supporting Suzie Scott, and Bill Graham, seen as the candidate of the majority of the executive. Graham won and went on to serve as president for five years, until 2000. Suzie Scott eventually returned to private law practice.

By raising dues and cutting expenses, the association managed to stabilize its finances for three or four years until the costs of the Olivieri case drained away the last of its reserves. By 2001, with no reserves, UTFA was nominally a quarter of a million dollars in debt, though already anticipating the substantial improvement that came in the following year with the university's half-million-dollar payment as part of the Olivieri settlement. And the years after that, 2003 to the present, have seen a dramatic rise in income so that reserves now are about two million dollars, and dues have been reduced from a high of 0.9% of annual salary to 0.75%. This change is the result of a dues checkoff recommended by a panel chaired by Alan Gold in 1997; the panel was set up as a part of a salary and benefits settlement mediated by Gold, and it was largely his skill and effort that persuaded the university to accept the Rand formula and agree to withhold UTFA dues from new faculty members. This award recognizes that the cost of achieving common benefits must be shared by all who benefit from them. The effects of the checkoff instituted in 1998 were not immediate, but as hundreds of new faculty members were hired in the last few years, replacing the great cohort of the 1960s as its members retired, the effects have been striking. Out of some 2600 potential members, the association collects dues from 2230; fewer than a dozen have opted to donate their dues to charity, and a dwindling number, some 370, of pre-Rand non-members remain.

With comparatively low inflation, salary and benefit settlements have allowed University of Toronto faculty to maintain, or slightly improve, their position relative to that of other professionals. The most recent settlement, arbitrated by Warren K. Winkler in 2006, gave faculty an across-the-board increase of 3% for 2005-06 and 3.25% for 2006-07. Winkler also rejected the university administration's argument that it could not afford to fully augment pensions to the rise in cost-of-living because the pension plan was in deficit. Actuarial surpluses and deficits, he wrote, were "snapshots" and should not be determinative. Most important, Winkler accepted the administration's own claim that Toronto was at "the top of the relevant market" in Canada, and therefore, he ruled, faculty compensation should reflect this.

One major change in the terms of faculty employment at the University of Toronto, a change the Faculty Association had long advocated, has just come about in 2006: the ending of mandatory retirement at age 65. Having opposed this for many years, the university administration rather suddenly changed its position and, in March 2005, agreed to terminate mandatory retirement as of July 1, 2006. It also agreed to a flexible plan for early retirement, allowing phased retirement over three years for faculty members between the ages of 58 and 66. The reasons for the administration's change of stand seem to have been first that the provincial government was about to abolish mandatory retirement in Ontario, and second that Toronto's arbitrary retirement policy was clearly leading to the loss of valuable senior faculty members who could continue to hold their positions at most other universities in North America.

Pensions have been at the centre of faculty and Faculty Association concern in recent years. In the 1990s there was a large and growing actuarial surplus in the university pension fund, the result of rising equity prices and, thus, apparently rising assets. For thirteen years from 1987 the university made no contribution to the pension fund, allowing some nine-hundred million dollars to be diverted to general purposes. While legal, this was imprudent; the money should have been put in a trust fund to be available when, as happened after 2000, the surplus rapidly disappeared, to be replaced by a massive actuarial deficit.

One effect of the stock boom of the late '90s was that, for a few years, defined contribution pension plans, nearly universal in the United States, seemed far superior to defined benefit plans such as the University of Toronto's. While Toronto faculty could look forward to retiring with 60 or 70 per cent of salary, many faculty in defined contribution plans were retiring with pensions equal to or greater than their salaries. A number of people active in UTFA argued vigorously for a defined contribution plan to be available at Toronto. With the fall in stock investment values after 2000, however, defined contribution plans lost much of their lustre. Many retired faculty with such plans saw their pensions fall by half or even more, and now the advocates of defined contribution seem to be mainly employers.

When the actuarial surplus was at its highest, some seven-hundred million dollars, a number of retired faculty members, believing that neither UTFA nor the university had acted sufficiently in their interest, got together to form RALUT (Retired Academics and Librarians at the University of Toronto). This was early in 2001, and the first president and principal spokesman of the group was Peter Russell, a distinguished recently retired member of the Political Science Department. RALUT's main focus was on pensions, and some of its members were persuaded that retired faculty had a legal claim to a major part of the pension surplus. The legal basis for this claim was never strong, and the surplus itself was merely a forecast, about to be drastically changed.

It was unfortunate that some of the organizers of RALUT chose to regard the Faculty Association as an antagonist, even threatening to sue UTFA for failure to represent their interests. And it was unrealistic to expect the university administration to negotiate directly with retired faculty. The administration's attitude was encapsulated in the remark of one senior Simcoe Hall functionary: "these people don't work here anymore." RALUT did succeed in focusing both the university administration and UTFA's attention on the problems of retired members, however, and gradually Peter Russell and George Luste managed to develop better relations between UTFA and RALUT.

So far as faculty pensions are concerned, however, both the diversionary interest in defined contribution schemes and the retired members' claim to a pay out from the pension surplus simply blurred the focus of pension demands and may well have prevented modest improvements in pension benefits while there still appeared to be a surplus.

Conclusion: Strengths and Weaknesses

The Faculty Association has both substantial strengths and serious weaknesses. To consider a few weaknesses first, its relations with the university administration depend on a voluntary agreement whose terms are unenforceable without the employer's goodwill. And the Memorandum of Agreement, negotiated a generation ago, is showing signs of age. The so-called "frozen policies" that may not be changed without agreement from both UTFA and the administration have proved to be too solidly frozen. To take one example: in 1999 an agreement was reached with the administration making significant changes in the appointments policy regarding tutors. Their titles were changed to Lecturer and Senior Lecturer and their appointments regularized following procedures used for tenure stream faculty. Most important, while not granting Senior Lecturers formal tenure, the administration did agree to "continuing appointments" that, in practice, provide security of tenure. It was a sensible agreement and a major improvement in appointments policy. But it had taken fourteen years of repeated efforts to negotiate.

Some matters, routinely dealt with in many certified union contracts, are not considered in the Memorandum of Agreement at all. The most important is faculty workload, already a pressing issue in some faculties and departments. The increasing disparity of salaries between the most and least "marketable" faculties is another issue ignored in the memorandum. And, of course, if a determined administration violates terms of the memorandum, UTFA may not take its case to the Ontario Labour Relations Board.

The Faculty Association has internal weaknesses: for many years its most active and, indeed, most useful members have come disproportionately from marginal groups, such as non-tenured members and former grievors. Less and less over the decades have established senior faculty taken an active part in UTFA affairs. Even the Annual General Meeting has been unable to entice more than a handful of members to attend. In six years of the past sixteen, including this year of 2006, the AGM has not had a quorum. Partly because of its narrow base of active members, the association's officers have tended to serve longer and longer terms. Bill Graham was president for seven years. A number of executive members have served a decade or more. This longevity of office, while threatening atrophy, does provide some strength of experience. And to expect a return to the days of Brough Macpherson and Bora Laskin is to ignore the fragmented, hurried, uncollegial university world of today.

The Faculty Association has two outstanding strengths: one arises from a major weakness in the governance of the university. Without a university senate or other truly representative body, the faculty relies, in times of trouble, on the Faculty Association as a defender of academic freedom, of decent employment practices, of university values generally. Its other strength lies in the quality of the people who have served and are serving the association, not all, incidentally within the university. For thirty years Jeffrey Sack has, always cogently and often brilliantly, negotiated for UTFA and, along with his colleague, Michael Mitchell, argued for faculty interests all the way from university tribunals to the Supreme Court of Canada.

To list those who have served their colleagues well on the executive, the council, committees, or in the UTFA office, would require more space than is available here. One must, however, remember two loyal servants of the association: Al Miller, a colleague from engineering, sometimes opinionated, often original, always honest, who died suddenly at the beginning of a meeting of the Executive Committee in April 1998. And Frank Madden, Director of Administration in the UTFA office, who died in March 2003, after fifteen years with the association. Even-tempered, good-humoured, always learning, always helpful, quietly wise, Frank was indispensable.

W.H. Nelson
October 2006

UTFA presidents since 1992:

Bill Graham, 1992-94;
Peter Boulton, 1994-95;
Bill Graham, 1995-2000;
Rhonda Love, 2000-02;
George Luste, 2002-

Preface

In the fall of 1990 I spoke to a Faculty Association group, mainly of Council members, on the history of the Association. Afterwards, several people urged me to put something in writing on this subject. I decided to do so, originally intending only to expand a little the points I had made in my talk. In order to do this, I felt I should look at some of the records on file in the Faculty Association office. As I delved into these materials, I began to realize how complex the Association's history was, how fragmentary its records were, how fragile its links with its past were becoming. Eventually I decided to attempt a much more substantial and general account than I had in mind at first. What follows is the result.

This kind of history is still new, and I found little to guide me in the way of other such accounts. It is a kind of institutional history that undoubtedly will develop rapidly in years ahead. It shares some of the characteristics of both university and trade union histories, but is quite different from either. For my written sources, I relied primarily on the records kept by the Faculty Association, and on materials available in the University of Toronto Archives. The UTFA (University of Toronto Faculty Association) records are mainly Minutes of the Executive Committee and some standing committees, Council Minutes, Minutes of Annual and other General Meetings, files of the

UTFA *Newsletter*, and some correspondence and miscellaneous materials. In general, UTFA materials are full and well-kept since 1977, broken and uneven for earlier times. There is some useful material for the 1950s, but little on the 1960s. Fortunately, the University Archives, though of little use after the mid-1970s, have considerable material from the 1950s, and, especially, the 1960s. Minutes of the Board of Governors and its committees, and Claude Bissell's Correspondence are particularly informative. In addition to these archival materials, I found material published by CAUT and OCUFA useful, as well as accounts in back files of the University of Toronto *Bulletin*.

For events, all of which are still within living memory, though some barely so, oral testimony is valuable. I talked with more than forty people who had been active in Association affairs, from R.M. Saunders, whose recollections of the Association go back to the early 1940s, to some members of the current UTFA Executive Committee. To list the names of all those who were kind enough to try to answer my questions would, however, be misleading. In many cases, I asked only a specific question or two, sometimes on a relatively minor point of fact. At the same time, there were many other people, important, at one time or another, in Association activities whom I did not consult, either because I felt I knew what I needed to know from earlier conversation, or because the written record was adequate. While oral statements are often superior in candour, immediacy, and vividness to what is written, they tend to be factually inferior. I found I had to be wary of recollections, including my own, when it came to detail and, especially, sequence.

I should, however, mention a few people whose views on important questions were valuable, and unobtainable in the written record. Jim Conacher was able to tell me a good deal about the Association in the late 1940s and early 1950s; he also kindly let me use material from an unpublished memoir of those times. I interviewed Jean Smith, Harvey Dyck, and Michael Finlayson at some length, because of the central roles they played as UTFA Presidents, in the 1970s and 1980s. Art Kruger's views were helpful, especially as he was active both in UTFA and in the University administration. Stan Schiff provided a special perspective as a long-time member of the UTFA Council.

The views of a few people other than those active in the Faculty Association were useful. Both Art Kruger and Milton Israel gave me some sense of the University administration's point-of-view in the negotiations leading to the Memorandum of Agreement. Ernest Sirluck's recollections of various crises in relations between the University administration and the Faculty Association were important. Bob Rae was able to answer some questions I had about the work of the Commission on University Government in 1969. Michiel Horn at York University generously shared with me some of the conclusions he had come to in his forthcoming study of university government in Canada; these were especially useful in clarifying faculty attitudes towards a dominant faculty role in university government in the 1960s, as well as in providing a basis for comparing Toronto attitudes on a number of matters with those elsewhere in the country.

Except as qualified from time to time, the terms "faculty" and "faculty member" in this work refer to people who do not hold administrative positions in the University other than that of department chair. Excluded, that is, are those who are excluded from faculty association membership in certified faculty unions. Most academic administrators, of course, at Toronto and elsewhere, value their professorial status and often resent not being seen as representatives of faculty opinion. Yet the reasons for denying their legitimacy as such representatives are compelling: they do not hold their administrative positions as faculty spokesmen, but as servants of the University, and if they bring faculty attitudes to their work, these must be subordinated, in case of conflict, to their primary institutional loyalty. If the faculty status of academic administrators ensured a faculty-run university, there would probably be no faculty associations and faculty unions.

Most of the people I mention in this work are, or were, professors; to use their academic titles would increase unnecessarily the length of the text, and probably diminish its interest. Similarly, for the sake of immediacy and a kind of authenticity, I usually use first names, often in their familiar forms—"Jim," "Bill," and "Mike." People mentioned in the text are properly identified in the Index. There are no footnotes; a copy of the text with citations to sources is on deposit in the office of the Faculty Association.

The UTFA staff, Frank Madden, Chris Penn, and, latterly, Allison Hudgins, were uniformly kind and helpful while I was working in the Association office, and later, in answering various questions. Bonnie Horne who, as President of UTFA, was frequently in the office while I was doing research there, was patient and generous in acquainting me with the current state of the Association, as well as in giving me her views of UTFA activities over the past decade. I am especially grateful to the UTFA Executive Director, Suzie Scott, for her support and encouragement, as well as her practical advice and assistance.

I owe thanks to three people in the History Department at Toronto: to Pat Yelle and Marion Harris for typing my manuscript and dealing good-humoredly with additions and revisions to it, and to Jennifer Francisco for further work in preparing the manuscript for publication. Lastly, I am grateful to Guy Allen for his indispensable help in the final editing and design of the book.

Anyone concerned with faculty association history is indebted, whether knowing it or not, to numbers of people who, even in a work as long as this, are mentioned only in passing or, more frequently, not at all. In the Toronto Association, in a half century, hundreds of members have chaired and served on committees, and served on Council. They and many others whose participation was less formal have given the Association its strength and purpose.

Preface

The Faculty Association commissioned this work, but the opinions in it are mine alone. I must also accept responsibility for its errors—errors of judgment which may be serious, but I hope not numerous; and errors of fact which may be numerous, but I hope not serious.

W.H. Nelson
University of Toronto

Chapter One
Early Days

Until 1954 the faculty association at the University of Toronto called itself "The Committee to Represent the Teaching Staff." A few old-timers faintly recall 1938 as the year it came into being, although its earliest surviving records seem to be for 1942. Certainly, while preceding by a few years similar faculty organizations at most Canadian universities, the Toronto organization is late by the standards of American universities or even by comparison with that at the University of British Columbia, which was formed in 1920 and was vigorous in pressing salary demands for a few years before subsiding in the 1930s into mere sociability.

The teaching staff at Toronto was not well-situated to organize in pursuit of common interests. Though large by the standards of the time, it was disparately distributed among the four old colleges, the Faculty of Arts and Science, and well over a dozen professional schools. Along with its horizontal division, the staff was sharply divided vertically by the academic hierarchy of the day. Indeed the Committee to Represent the Teaching Staff reflects these divisions: while its early organization and activities were notably casual in most respects, its representative character was precisely defined (though changed somewhat from time to time); in 1948, for example, the Committee had fourteen members representing ten constituencies— four from Arts and Science, one from each of the colleges, two from Medicine, four from the remaining professional faculties. As well, the hierarchical character of the staff was reflected in the seniority of virtually all the members of the Committee. It was a novelty when in 1949 Jim Conacher was elected to the Committee because his nominator, Edgar McInnis, thought there should be some representation for junior faculty.

Members of the CRTS were elected at an annual meeting of "the Teaching Staff of the University" which any member of the teaching staff could attend. In the late 1940s annual meetings were held, usually in November, in the Croft Chapter House. The Committee's Chairman would propose a Chairman for the following year, as well as nominees for vacancies on the Committee, and the meeting would acclaim these. Annual dues were collected in a hat that was passed around or left on the table. Dues were not excessive: in 1942 a collection of $14.35 had been taken up; in 1947 the Committee had a balance of 98 cents; even in 1952 when the Annual Meeting was attended by 207 members of staff, the collection of dues at the Meeting was only $139.55.

Other than the election of Committee members and a Chairman for the following year, the main business of the Annual Meeting was to hear and comment on the Chairman's report, and to endorse and occasionally propose matters to be dealt with in the next year. Until 1949 these did not include questions of salary, but focused rather on other benefits. In 1948, for example, the question of housing for new members of staff had been discussed, and the Chairman had agreed to try to get the student Housing Service made available to teaching staff; at the 1949 Meeting the Chairman announced that this had been done and that 71 faculty members had been assisted in finding housing. The 1948 Meeting also agreed to seek a group contract for medical care with Physicians' Services Incorporated. Other matters taken up in the late 1940s ranged from serious, if inconclusive, discussion of pensions to parking problems and the need for a faculty club.

It was the severity of postwar inflation that pushed the CRTS into cautious concern with salaries. The Annual Meeting in 1949 discussed the problem of inadequate salaries, especially for younger members of staff, and the Committee raised this question in a letter to Sidney Smith, the President of the University, in March of 1950. Specifically the Committee requested a raise in the salary scale for lecturers and assistant professors. In September Smith reported that the Finance Committee of the Board of Governors had asked him to make a definite proposal for a raise in the salary scale. In the months that followed there was some general discussion in Toronto of the plight of underpaid professors. The press sympathetically reported a resolution of students at University College offering to forego some of their own benefits so that their professors could be given pay increases. The *Globe and Mail* quoted President Smith's endorsement of the spirit of this offer and his assurance that the Board of Governors had been studying ways and means of raising salaries, though, he added, "we are not sure where the money is coming from."

In earlier years salaries had not been a major issue for several reasons: one was the habit of deference to authority, combined with an assumption of the general goodwill of those in authority. Another may have been a kind of professional academic reluctance to show excessive concern for money. Most important probably was the relative adequacy of academic salaries until the late 1940s. At Toronto, as at many other universities, academic salaries had been fairly stable between the wars. This meant, of course, that in the severely deflationary years of the 1930s the purchasing power of professors' salaries actually rose. A full professor in Toronto in the late 1930s could buy a substantial middle-class house in Rosedale with a year's salary; a similar house now would require perhaps eight years' salary. Or, if local changes in the cost of housing represent too extreme an example, a full professor could, in 1939, buy a new car in a middle price range

9

with two months' salary; a car of similar price status would now require three or four months' after-tax salary.

On the eve of the War average academic salaries at Toronto seem to have been about two-thirds those of a median of doctors', lawyers', and engineers' income. By the late 1940s this proportion had fallen to half. From July, 1946 to July, 1950 prices in Toronto rose about 35%; the salary scale at Toronto did not rise at all, though a minuscule "cost of living bonus" was paid ($144 in 1949). Finally, income taxes which had taken an average of 1.5% of pre-war income, took 12% in the late 1940s.

At the Annual Meeting of the teaching staff in November, 1950 a resolution was passed unanimously declaring it "urgent, in view of the continued and unabated rise in the cost of living, that there be an increase in salaries commensurate with that rise." The Committee, chaired by the eminent geophysicist, Tuzo Wilson, asked President Smith for an early meeting with him, telling him that the Annual Meeting had been exceptionally well-attended. Smith arranged a meeting early in January, 1951, the first of its kind, between himself, members of the CRTS and the Chairman, Vice-Chairman, and Finance Committee Chairman of the Board of Governors. These men, Col. W.E. Phillips, Mr. Henry Borden, and Mr. Walter Gordon, represented the old Board of Governors at perhaps both its best and worst. They were authoritarian and patronizing, but also occasionally protective in their attitude towards the University teaching staff. And, being at the centre of the Toronto financial and political establishment, they had power to make decisions.

After the meeting Professor Wilson wrote President Smith, thanking him rather effusively for having arranged the meeting, saying of the three members of the Board, how glad the Committee was "that these busy men could spare time to come." Smith replied that in sixteen years of administration he had never experienced such deep satisfaction as he had during the meeting. "The Chairman of the

Board of Governors and his colleagues," he wrote Wilson, "were greatly impressed by the fairness and yet the pointedness of the remarks of yourself and your colleagues." A few weeks later Smith announced a new salary scale, raising floors 40% for lecturers, down to 12% for full professors. It was a substantial increase, averaging over 20%, though it did not, of course, make up the 35% loss in purchasing power in the postwar years.

Faculty satisfaction at this salary increase did not last long. As a result of the Korean War, the rate of inflation rose in 1951 so that by the time of the Annual Meeting in November the cost of living was up 50% over 1946, a rise less than half of which was covered by the new salary rates. While the Meeting endorsed a resolution thanking the President and the Board for their attempt ("generous" was deleted from a first draft) to compensate staff for the effects of inflation, it called for a revision of salary scales until they were "at least equivalent in purchasing power to those of 1946."

In the spring of 1952 the Committee sent the President a series of tables and graphs showing the deterioration of faculty salaries in relation to the cost-of-living as well as in comparison with the income of other people in the work force. Thus, while university salaries fell further and further behind the rise in cost-of-living, most other wage earners, professional and non-professional, had increased their earnings more than the rise in prices. This graphic illustration of professorial decline represented the first of what was to be a series of similar statistical lamentations over the next forty years, unbroken until now. Like most such complaints that were to follow, it produced less than hoped-for results. One senses indeed a slight cooling in Sidney Smith's attitude to the CRTS; he did not repeat the experimental meeting with members of the Board of Governors. He did, it is true, address the Annual Meeting of staff in November, 1952, beginning what was to be for most of the next two decades an annual presidential appearance. And in February, 1953 he announced a new salary scale which, however, fell well below what the CRTS had asked for. The new salary scale ranged from $3,100 a year for lecturers to $7,200 for full professors (as against $2,000 to $5,500 pre-war).

Salaries were to continue to be a primary concern of the faculty organization at Toronto through the 1950s. Every year the CRTS, or after 1954, the new Association of the Teaching Staff, would ask the President to support faculty requests in his dealings with the Board of Governors. The President would reply courteously but evasively. The Board would eventually decide on salaries for the coming year; the President would announce this decision. The faculty association would usually thank the President for his efforts, often combining perfunctory gratitude with a solicitation for more next time. Once, it is true, after an 8% raise for 1955-56 at a time when inflation had temporarily abated, the Salary Committee of the Association "viewed with satisfaction the new salary schedule."

In April 1957 President Smith announced a substantial raise in salaries to be implemented over three years. The scale for lecturers was to be raised 57%; for assistant professors, 40%; for associate professors, 38%; and for full professors, 50%. These increases averaged 40% for the whole teaching staff: 16% in 1957-58, and about 11% in 1958-9 and 1959-60. By 1958 full professors at a salary floor of $10,000 had nearly regained the purchasing power of their $5,000 salaries of 1939. In 1959-60 Toronto professors actually moved about as much ahead of the rise in cost-of-living over the preceding twenty years as the rise in income tax.

In October, 1959 the Executive of the ATS heard that a comparison of Toronto salaries with those in American universities "reveals that Toronto fares extremely well indeed." Forgotten, if only for a moment, was the unredeemed decline of academic salaries in comparison with others: Canadian income as a whole had nearly *doubled* in purchasing power between 1939 and 1959, and this doubling was true of groups most easily comparable with professors, such as most

12

government employees and teachers. Even the favourable comparisons with American academic salaries are open to doubt, as a rather angry letter from Professor Adrian Brook to the ATS Chairman in March, 1960 makes clear.

With the possible exception of the initial campaign in 1950-51, the early efforts of the faculty association to influence salaries do not seem to have had much effect. The Board of Governors took other considerations more seriously—money available from the Provincial government and from endowments, income from tuition, special costs, and salary settlements elsewhere. As faculty salary submissions became an annual litany, it became that much easier, having ignored them one year, to do so again the next. Perhaps the most significant effect of regular faculty concern with salaries was gradually to sharpen and harden a sense of grievance as well as impotence, especially among younger members of staff.

Faculty organization at Toronto changed considerably during the 1950s and the major impetus for change came from outside, from the formation in 1951 of the Canadian Association of University Teachers (CAUT). The proposal for a national faculty association had come originally from the local association in Alberta in 1948. At the meetings of the Learned Societies in Kingston in 1950, at the instigation of a group from Alberta supported by some colleagues from Queen's, an organizing committee was set up and proposals for a constitution for a national body discussed. The organizers expected such an association to be based on individual membership like the American Association of University Professors (the AAUP, which already had some Canadian members). Toronto was represented at the Kingston discussions by Jim Conacher, who obtained the tentative support of the CRTS for such a national body. In June, 1951 at McGill the CAUT was formally launched, though its constitution was not finally adopted until the following year.

From the beginning the attitude of Toronto faculty towards the CAUT was ambivalent. The CRTS accepted Conacher's argument that, without a national organization, Canadian faculty might well be absorbed into the American Association of University Professors. And Toronto was sympathetic to the original aims of CAUT—the accumulation of national salary data and lobbying for federal funding of the universities. But a number of Toronto people were suspicious of a national association that might develop "trade union attitudes" or political objectives. Above all the CRTS wanted to prevent CAUT members at Toronto from forming a chapter independent of the CRTS itself. For a couple of years the CRTS had a sub-committee in charge of enrolling members in CAUT. But it became clear that if the local association was to control CAUT activities at Toronto it needed more formal organization itself. Out of this realization comes the re-organization of the Committee to Represent the Teaching Staff into the Association of the Teaching Staff (the ATS) in 1954.

In the fall of 1953 the CRTS sent out a questionnaire asking members of the teaching staff whether they wanted a formal association to represent them. There were 500 responses (from a total staff of 600); 72% were in favour; 18% were opposed but would support such an organization if it was formed; only 5% were flatly opposed. Within the CRTS there was some opposition to a new organization: it was argued that the "CRTS had proved effective," that "much might be lost" by setting up a new body, that a "loose organization was safer and more effective" than a formal one, that it was "confusing to have a constant shift of constitutions." Some claimed that such an association would resemble a trade union, and that the proposed dual membership with CAUT might eventually lead to the imposition of a national salary scale lower than Toronto's. Those in favour argued that a formal association would be more democratic than the CRTS, would be better able to safeguard essentials such as academic freedom, and would, with dual membership, resolve relations with CAUT. The questionnaire results really settled the argument, and in the spring of 1954 a constitution was drafted for the Association of the Teaching Staff, and adopted by the CRTS which dissolved itself, though most of its members simply became members of the Executive of the new body.

The first Annual Meeting of the ATS was on the first of December, 1954. Its highlight was an address by Sidney Smith who, as President of the University, gave his blessing to the new faculty association, noting that an association had a more permanent sound than a mere committee. He recalled his pleasant dealings with the CRTS: "In all my talks with the members of your executive, I have never once sensed the attitude of a bargaining agency"; rather, he continued (out of sight of land), we were "all in the same boat, rowing together, taking soundings, and charting our course." Smith avoided discussion of salaries, but did promise to consult the ATS about pension policy, and suggested that sixty-five was too low a retirement age. Later the meeting adopted a motion by Brough Macpherson that the ATS apply for group membership in the CAUT.

Although the association at Toronto has undergone some fairly substantial changes, the ATS of 1954 is recognizably the same body as the present University of Toronto Faculty Association (UTFA). The name was changed in 1972, and there have been a number of constitutional changes since, notably in 1976. But from 1954 Toronto has had a faculty association with a defined, dues-paying membership, and a constitution vesting power in an elected council as directed by an Annual Meeting or other general meetings. The name, though not the shape or functions of what is now the UTFA Council, is confusing before the mid-1960s; it was originally called the "Executive Committee" in the 1954 constitution of the ATS, and this committee was the successor of the old committee—the CRTS.

It was not until 1963 that the "Executive Committee" became the Council. However called, the Council has always been a body of members elected from the various faculties, schools, and colleges of the University. In the old CRTS, Arts and Science members, combined with those from the colleges, formed a majority. The ATS Council of 1954 sharply increased representation from the professional faculties; thus, while combined Arts and Science and college membership remained at eight (later raised to ten and then to twelve), the number of members from the professional faculties rose from six to sixteen (later raised to eighteen), so that each professional school or faculty would have at least one member. The result was a marked over-representation, until major reforms in 1976, of smaller professional schools. The extra weight, in the Council, of most of the professional faculties also made the Council often more conservative in outlook than the members-at-large.

With one notable exception, the scale and scope of the faculty association of the 1950s and even the 1960s was almost touchingly simple and small. The exception is attendance at Annual Meetings and other general meetings which, in the 1950s and 1960s, was frequently between 200 and 300; in the earlier years this represented a third or more of total University faculty. In recent years attendance at such meetings infrequently reaches 100—4% or so of total faculty. But in all other respects the present association is immensely larger— and certainly more expensive—than the old. Dues which now average close to $500 per year were inconsequential—$5 in 1957, of which $2.50 went to CAUT; $12 by 1961 with $10 going to CAUT. Even at this level there was grumbling at the amount of CAUT dues. Indeed in 1955 the ATS Executive complained that CAUT's then annual fee of $2 per member was too high!

With an income of only a few hundred dollars a year after payment of CAUT dues, the local association's expenses were necessarily slight (in December, 1955 the ATS had $606 in the bank; ten years later this balance was $1600). The only expense of any consequence was for stationery and mailing. For a number of years in the 1950s the largest annual expense other than for mailing was $15 for the annual Remembrance Day wreath. In 1959, incidentally, perhaps faintly foretelling a change in attitudes, the Chairman confessed the ATS had been unrepresented at the Memorial Services at Hart House, the Registrar having neglected to inform the association of this event.

Partly in consequence of having virtually no money, the Association of the 1950s and 1960s relied entirely on those unpaid volunteers who made up the Executive—the Chairman, the Vice-Chairman, the Secretary, and the Treasurer. To these should be added the chairmen and members of the standing committees: through the 1950s and early 1960s there were three of these—Salary, Pension, and Policy committees. Meetings varied in frequency; committees often met monthly; the Council had six or eight meetings a year; from 1959 on, following a proposal by Jim Conacher, there was a Spring as well as an annual Fall general meeting of the ATS. The Association had no office of its own; its headquarters in a given year were in the Secretary's University office. As early as 1963, Bora Laskin, who was then Chairman, asked the University to provide office space for the ATS, but received no reply.

By the mid-1960s the increasing business of the Association was beginning to put a particular burden, not yet on the Chairman, but on the Secretary, who kept minutes and handled correspondence and mailings. In 1965 there was some discussion of released time for the Secretary. Then in 1967 the Association hired its first regular employee; this was Mrs. Geraldine Sandquist who was to be the Association's sole employee, always part-time, for the next nine years. In the spring of 1959 the Association had bought a filing case—putting off to that fall the more momentous purchase of a typewriter. For some years this modest equipment moved from one secretary's office to the next. When Gerry Sandquist started work, George Duff who was then Chairman was able to find her a little office in the Mathematics Department which served as the Association headquarters until 1969 when the University finally made modest quarters available in the Tip Top Building.

Until late in the 1960s the character of the Toronto faculty association was markedly different from that of later years. It was very much a professors' organization, not only underfunded and casual in its operations, but resolutely amateurish, and usually uncritical of the paternalism of the day. Through the 1950s the concerns of the association were narrowly confined to salary and other benefits. To these was added in the 1960s a growing interest in faculty participation in governing the University. Even here, however, the faculty association seems to have been much more interested in finding an enlarged faculty role in the University hierarchy than in challenging the hierarchy. The President of the University, whether Sidney Smith in the 1950s or Claude Bissell in the 1960s, invariably addressed the Annual Meeting, and was received with deference. Frequently, indeed, the date of the Annual Meeting was determined by the President's availability.

Most of the officers of the Association in these years, and virtually all the Chairmen, were senior members of staff, sometimes eminent scholars, more often perhaps eminent University personages. A striking difference from the practice of later times lay in the dominance of the natural sciences and mathematics. During the twenty years from 1948 to 1968 the Association was led by a Chairman from mathematics or natural science for twelve years, by someone from one of the professional faculties for five years and by an Arts professor for only three years. In contrast, during the past twenty years, there has been a President from one of the natural sciences for only one year while the Association has had a President from an Arts department for sixteen years (for ten years, indeed, from History).

The natural scientists who used to dominate the Association were often formidable Department heads like G.B. Langford in Geology, C.R. Myers in Psychology, and K.C. Fisher in Zoology. Some were, or were to be, University administrators like F.E.W. Wetmore in Chemistry. The dominance in the Association of natural scientists extended to the Executive as well. In 1957-58, for example, all four representatives from Arts and Science were from Science departments. Some of the departments these men came from, incidentally, have in more recent times often been noticeably hostile to faculty militance. Zoology, for example, for some years had the lowest proportion of UTFA members of any Arts and Science department, and Chemistry has been a predictable centre of opposition to many UTFA actions; yet in the 1950s these were among the most active centres of faculty association activity in the University.

There were, to be sure, among the old Chairmen of the Association some truly eminent scholars—Tuzo Wilson (although he was also very much part of the University scientists' establishment), Bora Laskin in Law, and Brough Macpherson in political science. But it seems likely their roles in the faculty association were determined more by their University standing than by their scholarly standing. There seem to have been several reasons for the prominence of established senior men in the old faculty association. First, it was a hierarchical University, in which junior or unknown members of the teaching staff could not carry much weight. The faculty association as an organization had no power at all—no collective agreement, no regular procedures for discussion, no negotiations. Its only hope of affecting University policy was through the personal influence, mediation perhaps, of senior professors. Finally, senior professors themselves appear often to have had some sense of obligation towards their weaker and younger colleagues, this of course, another aspect of the vanished paternalism of the day.

The old faculty association was also, as one would expect, very much a man's world. It is not that women had no role, but that their role was circumscribed by the same conventions that limited their role in the University. For a good many years, the years when the Association had virtually no money, it was a convention for the Treasurer to be a woman. For seven or eight years, indeed, one woman, Edna Park from the Faculty of Household Science, served as Treasurer, until in 1963 Bora Laskin ushered her into Association history with a courtly little speech of gratitude. Women served on standing committees, though they did not chair them. In 1954 and again in 1955 two of the seven members of the Salary Committee were women. Women's issues were occasionally raised, though usually in the form of a question that went unanswered as when, in 1954, Brough Macpherson, then Chairman of the Policy Committee, posed the question, "Is there any discrepancy in salary between male and female members of the University staff?"

Women members were sometimes expected to, or allowed to, address their own issues, as when in 1954 a women's committee took up the question of group insurance for women faculty; eight years later, however, the group life insurance policy available to women without dependents was still for $1000, while the men's policy had been extended to cover up to three years' salary. The Association was certainly aware of salary and benefits differences between men and women. A pension study in 1961, for example, expected 38 members of the teaching staff, 24 men and 14 women, to retire between 1960 and 1965 at the then retirement age of 68. The men were expected to receive average annual pensions of $4890, representing 40% of average final salaries of $12,250. The women were expected to receive pensions averaging $2800, 32% of final salaries of $8750.

When injustice towards the vulnerable, whether women, or junior members of staff, or pensioners, was noted, it was usually brought to the attention of the University administration, that is, the President, and then forgotten for a while. In these equity issues, as in the general question of benefits, the Association felt itself helpless, unless, of course, it were to behave like a trade union and attempt to bargain collectively. For the senior academics who dominated the Association through the 1950s and 1960s to do this was simply unthinkable, unprofessional. There is, to be sure, a slow but perceptible decline in deference in these years. When, in the spring of 1955, President Sidney Smith invited the ATS Executive to dinner, one member demurred, saying "it should be an individual payment dinner." This tiny flicker of independence was clearly regarded by the rest of the Executive as eccentric, but, within a decade the ATS was beginning to distance itself from the President's offers of hospitality.

Similarly the tone of Association overtures to and responses from the University administration began to change in the early 1960s. By 1961 the complacence of Toronto faculty about their salaries had faded again; salaries were "no longer adequate" especially when an Annual Meeting that year was told that while Toronto salaries averaged $8900, the average at Harvard was $13,800. When Howard Rapson, a genial chemical engineer and invariable friend of the University administration, moved that the Association express appreciation for recent salary increases, his motion was defeated. The Spring Meeting in 1963 did pass a motion of appreciation to the President and Board of Governors for the improved salary scale (a 7% increase for 1963-64), but only after accepting by nearly two-to-one an amendment expressing "its disappointment with the slightness of the increase."

It is easy now to be impatient with what appears to be the caution, the timidity, the obsequiousness of faculty attitudes a generation ago. Partly, of course, this is simply a matter of changed conventions of language and behaviour. We now observe a set of conventions of language in regard to women, to race, to culture, to youth and age and established authority which are as precise and often as meaningless as the different conventions of a generation past. Those conventions tended to show respect for authority, for seniority, for ceremony, for corporate tradition and order. Our conventions now pay lip-service, at least, to freedom, individualism, and, above all, to social equality.

Slackness of thought and pure hypocrisy live as harmoniously with
current conventions as with those of the past. Contrariwise, clearminded people with decent values were able to work effectively within
the old conventions as they are within the new.

Still, if one must choose, our current university conventions are
surely less stultifying than those they replaced. When Claude Bissell
was installed as President of the University of Toronto in 1958, there
were two days of ceremonial exercises—public lectures, lunches,
breakfast with student leaders, interminable speeches. In his memoir
of his university days Bissell recalls Donald Creighton's welcoming
speech—"a small masterpiece, dancing with wit and shrewdness," in
which Creighton described the University with elaborate metaphor as
an empire held together by feudal institutions and loyalties. If one
reads Creighton's words now, across a gulf of time, they seem la-
boured, contrived, sometimes downright silly. His duchies and
knights, fiefs and bishops, his ponderous imperial nostalgia, all seem
pompous, heavy and irrelevant. After all, under this panoply was
much that was simply insensitive, parochial, stolidly authoritarian. It
was not ceremonial loyalties that held together the University, but the
hard-fisted management of a handful of Toronto businessmen with
close connections to the Tory party. Yet it was this world, both real
and ideal, that Toronto faculty of a generation ago had to live in.

Chapter Two
University Government—
Faculty Power

Universiity government became the overriding preoccupation of the Toronto faculty association during the 1960s. The prospect of faculty participation in running the University had not been seriously considered before 1960, and ceased to be a practical concern after 1971. But for a time during the 1960s a major faculty role in University government seemed to offer a way of transcending the traditional limits on faculty influence at Toronto while, at the same time, avoiding the prospect of a mere employee-employer relationship between faculty and the University.

Many Toronto faculty members knew, of course, that professors in English and Australian universities as well as in some of the great American universities took part in governing their institutions. But this was not a Canadian tradition and at Toronto, especially, habitual conservatism as well as the complexity of the relationship among the colleges, the Faculty of Arts and Science, and the professional faculties, had discouraged reform. The long-established practice by which faculty members dominated academic decision-making while the President and the Board of Governors handled University finances had seemed to work, at least until the late 1950s. What changed in the 1960s was, first and most important, the massive expansion of the University. The size of the faculty and the student body was to double in a few years with a much larger proportionate increase in the number of graduate students. This was after a long period of relative stability. The old institutional structures of the University simply could not adapt to this explosion of numbers.

Expansion doomed the casual intimacy of the old University. The kind of influence, informal but substantial, which senior professors had had was smothered by the sheer size of the new University. Inevitably the University developed an increasingly bureaucratic administration, more and more out-of-reach of the faculty. This, in turn, threatened, or seemed as if it might threaten, established professorial rights and immunities. Academic freedom itself seemed less secure in this new climate. Here the activities of the CAUT in behalf of academic freedom, initially in response to the Crowe case at United College in Winnipeg, gradually penetrated even Toronto's conservatism. In all this, of course, Toronto shares the experiences of most other Canadian universities of the time. There was at Toronto, however, one additional influence for reform: that was the new President, Claude Bissell.

Bissell came back to Toronto as President in 1958 after a couple of years as President at Carleton University. He had been Sidney Smith's assistant for a number of years and knew how the University was run. He thought he could get along with Eric Phillips, the dominating Chairman of the Board of Governors, and had no initial intention of challenging Colonel Phillips's tight control of the University budget.

Smith, of course, had gone to Ottawa as John Diefenbaker's Minister of External Affairs, a position for which he was poorly prepared and in which he was to serve with considerable, if diminishing, ineptitude until his sudden death early in 1959. Smith had been popular with the Toronto faculty. Early suspicions of him as a Tory politician brought in to serve the interests of the Tory provincial government and the Tory Board of Governors gave way to an appreciation of his diligence, good humour, and apparent commitment to the interests of the University. Whatever his weaknesses on the national political scene, Smith had been a successful University politician. He not only knew who everyone was, he knew what everyone wanted. He was ebullient, disarmingly folksy, reassuring, encouraging, liberal and expansive in manner. He was also platitudinous, superficial and often devious. His apparent agreement with faculty concerns, either individual or collective, was nicely balanced by a convenient memory. Bissell recalls a friend's comment that Smith was "not nearly so amiable as he appears to be." Nevertheless, he was popular, and a few months after his departure to Ottawa, the faculty association brought him back for a daylong tribute.

Bissell was, in manner and temperament, as different from Sidney Smith as could easily be imagined. While Smith was bluff and outgoing, Bissell was shy and somewhat introspective, never much at ease with people he did not know well and like. He enjoyed private merriment and was witty with intimates, but never mastered the political art of appearing to enjoy himself when he did not. Most older faculty members at Toronto now recall Bissell with high regard. For one thing, in the markedly unprofessorial procession of Toronto presidents over the past sixty years—an Anglican cleric, a lawyer-politician, two medical research-administrators, an electrical engineer and, finally, another lawyer—Bissell stands out as an Arts and College man, a humanist. It is true, of course, that as President, Bissell was more at ease with the professional faculties and their affairs than with the Faculty of Arts and Science. But it is probably more a sign of than a reproach to his humanism that he found the minutiae of Arts and Science Faculty Council business—curricular prescription and the academic standing of students—boring.

It is the conventional wisdom of most of those at Toronto who remember the Bissell years that he was a successful, some would say a luminously successful, President during his first nine years in office until he went to Harvard for a year in 1967-68 as the first Mackenzie

King Professor of Canadian Studies. In this view, Bissell's final three years as President, from 1968 to 1971, were years of comparative failure which took away some of the lustre of earlier times. This is a somewhat shallow judgment, both in its uncritical approval of Bissell's first years and in its unsympathetic dismissal of his last. It was the times that changed; Bissell had little more control of the surge of events in the University world in the early 1960s than he did at the end of the decade. His first years in office were years of unprecedented expansion with, in contrast to the times that preceded or followed, limitless funds for new staff, new programmes, new buildings.

It is probably true that Bissell's talents were better suited to the early stages of expansion than to the later. He was imaginative and innovative in sketching out preliminary plans for a new and vastly larger university. He was especially successful in combining reform with expansion in the major professional faculties. With Arts and Science he was less successful, partly because of the difficult problem of the old Colleges, clinging to their academic autonomy and delaying any rational expansion of arts and science as a whole. Consequently the growth of arts and science, apart from the development of the School of Graduate Studies under Ernest Sirluck's deanship and the eventual building of the Robarts Library, tended to be largely quantitative only—a doubling and then often a second doubling of departmental staff without much reference to the special needs of strong and weak areas. To this day the absence of a coherent vision of expansion in arts and science is all-too-well preserved in steel and concrete in the dreary row of academic buildings on the west side of St. George Street, the worst of them unsurprisingly the Arts building, Sidney Smith Hall, still startling in its ugliness and inutility after thirty years.

Bissell certainly was, in his origins and preferences, far more a faculty man than the presidents who preceded and followed him. He understood faculty concerns easily and, in turn, was easily trusted by faculty members. It is true, of course, that through most of his working life Bissell was an administrator rather than scholar or teacher. Inevitably he was most sympathetic to two kinds of professor—the pure scholar, and the academic administrator. For members of the faculty association who took an adversarial attitude towards the University administration he had little sympathy. Fortunately for him, the faculty association during most of his presidency shared his view of a general identity of interest between faculty and administration. Indeed, the faculty association's interest in a faculty role in University government reflected this cooperative attitude, as did Bissell's support for such a role.

A few in the faculty association had been vaguely interested in a role in university government for years. At a meeting of the ATS Executive in 1955, Ken Fisher, then Chairman, asked rhetorically "whether it would be at all feasible in the future to think of one of the Executive being on the Board of Governors." Fisher went on to point out "that the President really appreciates the work of the Association." The wistful linking of an ambition to share modestly in the rule of the University with a claim to Presidential approval is revealing. For the most part, however, the ATS in the late 1950s was not much interested either in University government or in issues of academic freedom. It was the CAUT's response to the Crowe case at United College which joined these two subjects and gradually brought both to the grudging attention of the Toronto Association.

As mentioned earlier, the ATS had been organized in 1954 partly, at least, in an attempt to control and limit CAUT activities at Toronto. The original suspicion of Toronto faculty towards the CAUT continued. From 1955 on CAUT activists had been committed to establishing a national office and probably having a permanent secretary. The Toronto association opposed this. In 1957, for example, W.G. Raymore, a past Chairman, wrote the new ATS Chairman, C.R. Myers, asking of CAUT, "What will a full-time secretary have to do to keep him busy? Why does CAUT need a National office? What is it for? What would it do?" At about the same time, the Toronto Association reprimanded CAUT for proposing direct pre-election lobbying of political parties on the question of federal funding for the universities. Indeed, the ATS was particularly hostile to any CAUT activity that could be interpreted as political, and its initial response to the Crowe case reflected this.

The Crowe case, of course, precipitated the establishment of a national office for CAUT, along with, eventually, a set of procedures for dealing with questions of academic freedom and also a CAUT commitment to the reform of University government. The facts of the Crowe case are well-known, are, indeed, now an essential part of the history of academic freedom in Canada. Harry S. Crowe was a young history professor at United College in Winnipeg (now the University of Winnipeg) who, in 1958, was dismissed by the College Board of Regents for remarks he had made in a personal letter to a colleague. The letter had apparently been found by someone who gave it to the College principal, W.C. Lockhart, who proceeded somewhat shamelessly to publicize its contents, finally bringing it officially to the attention of the Board. In his letter Crowe showed mild irreverence towards the United Church and to some of the ministers of that church on the United College teaching staff, as well as more pointed disapproval of the businessmen on the Board of Regents of the College. Eventually seventeen members of the teaching staff resigned in support of Crowe.

The CAUT, which had not hitherto investigated abuses of academic freedom, followed the long-established practice of the American Association of University Professors and appointed a fact-finding committee to go to Winnipeg. This ad hoc committee was composed of two professors, Vernon Fowke of the University of Saskatchewan and Bora Laskin from the University of Toronto. Their report exonerated Crowe of any wrong-doing, castigated Principal Lockhart for his invasion of personal privacy in his use of the Crowe letter, and concluded that the Board of Regents had dismissed Crowe without reasons and without a hearing. The Board's action constituted "an unjust and unwarranted invasion of the security of academic tenure." Crowe's only crime, the Fowke-Laskin Committee concluded, was that he "was not sufficiently complaisant, not servile enough in thought and attitude to his administrative superiors."

The Crowe case and, especially, the Fowke-Laskin Committee's report quickly became a matter of national interest. The press, and probably the public as well, was divided on the issues the case raised. On the one hand, conservatives were uneasy at the lack of deference to authority that Crowe and those colleagues who supported him had shown. But, on the other hand, the strident anti-intellectualism and complacent arrogance of the businessmen who dominated the Board of Regents at United College did raise questions even among some conservatives about the suitability of businessmen as university overseers. And Principal Lockhart's vacillations and devious self-importance did little to reassure the public about the effectiveness of internal university management. Within the academic community in Canada sentiment among younger faculty, especially Arts faculty, was overwhelmingly in support of Crowe and the CAUT. Among university administrators and senior faculty, especially in the professional faculties, some had reservations about Crowe, but hardly any supported the United College Board or Principal.

At Toronto there was considerable faculty support for Crowe and his like-minded colleagues, led by the History Department. But the faculty association was nervously cautious. When the CAUT appointed the Fowke-Laskin Committee, the ATS Chairman, still C.R. Myers, wrote to Clarence Barber at Manitoba, the President of CAUT, complaining that CAUT's action might damage its appearance of impartiality and discretion. Early in 1959 the CAUT circulated a questionnaire on academic freedom to local faculty associations throughout the country. Dick Saunders, who was Chairman of the Policy Committee and about to succeed Myers as ATS Chairman, assured CAUT that academic freedom was perfectly secure at Toronto, that no cases threatened its enjoyment, and that the President of the University could adequately protect the freedom of the faculty.

This was a curious reply, considering that one of the most dangerous attacks on academic freedom in Canada before the Crowe case had been the sustained effort by a majority of the Toronto Board of Governors to bring about the dismissal of Frank Underhill for his criticisms of Britain and the British Empire between 1939 and 1941. Underhill had been at that time and for many years afterward Saunders's colleague in the History Department. It is true that Canon Henry Cody, as President of the University, did finally support Underhill, but only after he had earlier recommended his dismissal. It was not the President, but rather pressure from outside the University that saved Underhill's job and with it, though rather precariously, academic freedom at Toronto.

The Toronto Association's hostility to CAUT support for Crowe and his colleagues continued through 1959. The ATS protested when the CAUT placed an advertisement in the *Times Literary Supplement* advising applicants for positions at United College to contact the CAUT Secretary before proceeding with their applications. Then the CAUT appointed J.H. Stewart Reid as its first Executive Secretary. Reid had been Chairman of the History Department at United College and one of the first to resign in support of Crowe. At Toronto, Myers, the retiring ATS Chairman, wrote to his successor, Saunders, that although he thought Reid "is a very fine person," his CAUT appointment was a terrible mistake: "The implication of this will be that C.A.U.T. has been captured by the Crowe faction at United." The ATS Executive discussed the numerous letters of protest it had received concerning Reid's appointment; these contained "no criticism of his qualifications," but "it is strongly felt that the CAUT executive was in error in appointing a person who was so closely linked with the controversy at United College."

At the Spring General Meeting in 1959 there was considerable objection to a strong CAUT supporter, Jim Eayrs, even reporting to the Meeting on matters connected with the Crowe case. Later in the year the ATS Executive voted down a proposal from CAUT to solicit voluntary contributions from members to help reimburse people who had paid their own expenses in support of CAUT's investigation into the Crowe case. At a November meeting, after setting the date of the Annual Meeting "at the convenience of the President to attend," the Executive rejected a CAUT proposal for the adoption of a detailed statement of principles concerning academic freedom and tenure like that which the AAUP had had in place for many years. At Toronto, the Executive concluded, "no explicit definition of 'academic freedom and tenure' was appropriate." Finally, in January 1960 the Executive shelved a motion to invite Stewart Reid to the Spring Meeting.

The controversy over the Crowe case died down in 1960 and, rather suddenly and quietly, the Toronto Association began to move towards the CAUT position. A "University Government" sub-committee of the Policy Committee was set up and later made into a standing committee of the Association. Within a year or so a new group began to dominate the ATS. In this group were people like Brough Macpherson and Jim Conacher who had supported the CAUT for years, along with people who had not hitherto been prominent in association activities, such as Jim Eayrs, Larry Lynch, and Bora Laskin. Except for Laskin, these new ATS activists were from Arts departments—Macpherson and Eayrs from Political Economy, Conacher from History, Lynch from Philosophy. And, in the early 1960s, the senior professors from the natural sciences who had dominated the faculty association since the War began to fade from the scene.

The first report, in December, 1960, of the Committee on University Government, chaired by Larry Lynch, was a straightforward and, by Toronto standards, a radical criticism of the governing structure of the University. The report noted that the traditionally undemocratic and authoritarian character of university government in Canada was under general attack. Faculty associations at Saskatchewan, the University of British Columbia, and Manitoba had recommended that elected academic staff constitute half the membership of their governing boards. The CAUT was recommending that faculty members constitute a majority on governing boards. McMaster already had two elected staff members on its Board. And, of course, universities in Britain and Australia had long had faculty representatives on governing bodies. Lynch's committee proposed that there be at Toronto eight elected faculty members (out of twenty-four) on the Board of Governors, that faculty members should share equally with the Board of Governors in the choice of a President, and that deans be selected by committees of their faculty councils.

The Board of Governors took no serious notice of the faculty association's new ambitions. Eric Phillips was still Chairman and was implacably opposed to faculty representation. The Board's argument was that its management of the University, especially of its finances, was disinterested, and that faculty representatives on the Board would find themselves in a conflict of interest and would introduce factious and partisan issues. Bissell, however, was sympathetic to the idea of faculty representation on the Board. He not only grasped the increasing irrelevance of the old separation between academic and financial matters, but saw reform of the Board as likely to strengthen the power of the President. He was less sympathetic to faculty requests for a larger role in making internal appointments. In appointing chairmen, he wanted to rely on anonymous advisory committees of his own choice, and he wanted to continue to appoint deans without the advice of any committee. He objected also to any limitation on the length of administrative terms of office.

The faculty association's commitment to the reforms first advocated in Lynch's 1960 Report had been strengthened, however, by an ATS poll of the whole faculty released early in 1963. This showed 90% of the faculty supported the proposal for faculty representation on the Board of Governors, and 80% supported a formal faculty role in choosing presidents, deans, and chairmen. With no prospect, for the moment, of representation on the Board, the ATS concentrated on the other question. In a meeting with Bissell in September, 1964, Jim Conacher pressed him for action, and in November Bissell yielded. He set up an advisory committee, chaired by R.E. Haist, a physiologist in the Medical Faculty, to consider new procedures in making academic appointments and in defining tenure, as well as procedures for appointing chairmen, deans, and directors.

Of the twelve members of the Haist Committee, only Conacher had been active in the faculty association's work on university government reform, but the Committee accepted his guidance, and the Haist Rules that finally emerged in 1967 from the Committee's work substantially embodied faculty association proposals. Tenure was now to be recommended by faculty-dominated committees. "Heads" became "Chairmen," and were to be selected for (renewable) five-year terms by committees, a majority of whose members would be faculty members not themselves in administration. And deans were to be selected by a similar process. The Haist Rules, though modified since—student members, for example, were added to the selection committees for deans in 1971—still determine the basic process of making academic appointments at Toronto. Indeed, the Haist Rules represented the faculty association's one major success in the 1960s in gaining a serious role for faculty in the internal management of the University.

The CAUT, in the meantime, had been pressing for a national commission to examine university government. In 1962-63 Bissell was president of the Association of Universities and Colleges of Canada, an association largely of university presidents and administrators, and was able to persuade that body to join with the CAUT in establishing such a commission. Bissell became chairman of a joint steering committee to set up the commission. The steering committee eventually settled on two commissioners, Sir James Duff, the retired vice-chancellor of the University of Durham, and Robert Berdahl, a young American political scientist who had written a book about the governing of British universities.

The Duff-Berdahl Report, when it was released early in 1966, offered, predictably, a British solution for the problems of Canadian university government—reformed and strengthened faculty senates in control of academic policy, and substantial faculty representation on governing boards. In the years that followed, most English Canadian universities reformed their governing structures along the lines proposed by Duff-Berdahl, with the addition of student representatives on senates and governing boards, an issue that emerged just after the release of the Report.

At Toronto, however, reform was to move in a different direction, and Claude Bissell's views were here of critical importance. Bissell disliked the authoritarian finality of the Board of Governors, which he saw as essentially reflecting an American view of university government. But he also had misgivings about the cumbersome and measured constitutionalism of British university government. In 1951 he had spent some months in England on a Carnegie Foundation grant examining British university government, and had found it a "dispiriting experience." He was not only offended by the smugly patronizing attitude of senior administrators at the provincial English universities, but thought British practices inappropriate to the pace and politics of the expanding universities of Canada. He wondered whether there might not be a Canadian solution to the problems of running Canadian universities, a system of "pragmatic and tempered absolutism" that would reflect the "Canadian emphasis on directness and decisiveness." By the time the Duff-Berdahl Report was released, Bissell had decided that what Toronto, at least, needed was not a reformed Board of Governors and a reformed Senate, but a new representative, unitary body combining the financial powers of the Board with the academic responsibilities of the Senate.

The idea of a unicameral university governing body was considerably discussed in a number of Canadian universities in the late 1960s and, indeed, tentatively adopted in reforms proposed at the University of Waterloo. Waterloo eventually abandoned the project for unitary government, and only at Toronto was it eventually implemented. To be fair to Bissell and to those who supported his proposal for unitary government in the university, his concept was more sophisticated and complex than the naked unicameralism that developed out of it. It seems likely that Bissell's views were reinforced by his experience with an advisory body which he created in 1965, partly in response to faculty association pressure for a greater faculty role in university government. This was the President's Council, wholly advisory to the President and with no statutory power, whose members were drawn from the Board of Governors, the University administration and the faculty.

Despite its informal character, the President's Council carried great weight. It freely discussed matters which cut across the traditional division between the Board of Governors' supervision of finances and the Senate's control of academic policy—largely matters arising from the rate of University expansion, such as the ramifications, academic and financial, of new faculty appointments, and the ever closer relations with government. Bissell invited the faculty association to supervise elections for the five (later raised to seven) faculty representatives on the President's Council, and several ATS activists, including Larry Lynch and Brough Macpherson, were among those first elected to it. For the first time, in 1965 and 1966, the ATS had the heady experience of skirting the edges of real power in the University.

There was, of course, a threat of co-option here. Indeed, from Bissell's point-of-view, to involve faculty representatives in University planning and decision-making was, not only to make use of them, but to disarm them. Some ATS members were suspicious of the President's Council and wished to distance the ATS from it. John Crispo proposed that members of the President's Council be required to resign from the ATS Council. But Howard Rapson, who had been elected to the President's Council, saw no conflict of interest in membership on both bodies. Brough Macpherson, however, was Chairman of the ATS in 1965 when he was elected to the President's Council, and promptly resigned his chairmanship.

For its part, the Board of Governors was also suspicious of the President's Council, as well as of Bissell's interest in University reform. Eric Phillips had finally given up his long and dominating chairmanship, but the Board remained a very conservative and increasingly anachronistic body. In 1965 it was composed of eight lawyers, thirteen business executives, four (retired) politicians, and two others— an editor and a scientist; the President and the Chancellor of the University were also members, ex officio. Although members of the Board were appointed for renewable six-year terms, most of them died in office. In 1965 sixteen members had served for more than twenty years, and the average age of Governors was sixty-four. Bissell told the ATS that only one senior member of the Board was sympathetic to faculty representation. Nevertheless, after the release of the Duff-Berdahl Report early in 1966 the Board invited three members of the President's Council to sit on the Board as observers. Two of these were expected to be elected academic staff members. Later in

1966 the President's Council approved in principle faculty representation on the Board.

By this time even the Tory Toronto *Telegram* was able to approve the presence of faculty observers on the Board of Governors, noting patronizingly that there were many faculty members, especially senior administrators, "who could perform just as capably on their university's board of governors, as some of the governors from business themselves." It seemed as if a major role for faculty members in the governance of the University was imminent.

At this point, however, the rise of a radical and ambitious movement for student power complicated the question of university government reform. Within two years, from 1966 to 1968, the radical student movement at Toronto became a formidable force. Bissell had had a few skirmishes with student leaders before going off to Harvard for the 1967-68 academic year, but had felt he could contain and divert student protest without bringing students into the management of the University. While at Harvard he changed his mind, to a considerable degree because of the terrifying student riots at Columbia University in the spring of 1968.

To a university president the most frightening thing about the affair at Columbia was the final aimlessness and helplessness of the administration after its initial insensitivity had alienated most of the student body and many members of the academic staff. Bissell was determined to prevent the Columbia syndrome from developing at Toronto. He thought he could drive a wedge between student "radicals" and those he called "revolutionaries" by involving the former in the reform of the University's governance and by inviting student leaders to take a major role in the structures that reform was to create.

While Bissell was at Harvard, the President's Council had endorsed the establishment of a commission to recommend changes in the government of the University, and as soon as he returned, in June, 1968, Bissell persuaded the Board of Governors to approve such a commission. Reluctantly the Board abandoned its original view that such a commission should be merely advisory to the Board itself. It would instead make its own recommendations and include student and staff representatives as well as representatives of the Board.

The Students Administrative Council balked at the proposal for equal representation of students, staff, and governors, and proposed that the Commission should have four members each from the student body and the teaching staff, two representatives from the Board and the President, the Board members and the President without voting rights. The students also proposed that alumni and administrative representation be abandoned. Bissell thought the student demand for the disfranchisement of Board members was a negotiating stance, but agreed to an increase in the number of student and staff representatives to four each. This formula was endorsed by the President's Council and by the ATS Executive. Bissell thought he could persuade the Board to accept the increased number of student and staff representatives, but he was uneasy about it, since he had already offended some governors by talking indiscreetly to the press about the advantages of a unitary government.

Although his main concern was with the attitude of the Board and the student leaders, Bissell also worried a little about the faculty. While still at Harvard in the spring of 1968, he considered making a direct request to the faculty association for its support on the reform of the governance of the University. He raised this matter confidentially in a letter to Frances Ireland, his executive secretary on whose advice he frequently relied. She, however, strongly discouraged his proposed approach to the ATS, and recommended instead that he rely on the faculty members of the President's Council for support. The faculty association, she wrote him, "is awfully democratic and slow-moving," and, in a reference to that year's ATS Chairman, "Mike Grapko ain't no Macpherson."

Bissell dropped the idea of trying to work closely with the ATS on university government, though he was concerned about the young, recently arrived Americans on the teaching staff and their closeness in outlook to the student radicals. On the whole, however, he thought he could rely on faculty support. The ATS Executive had approved his formula for representation on a University Government Commission, and its approval by a Special General Meeting of the faculty association called for October 3, 1968 seemed only a formality.

Chapter Three

University Government—
Faculty Failure

The faculty association at Toronto has never, before or since, over so long a time, been as active, as busy, as engaged, as it was during the year-and-a-half from October, 1968 to the end of March, 1970. There were, during this time, eleven general meetings of the ATS. They were variously attended, but most were full of excitement and a sense of important matters hanging in the balance. The sheer number of meetings had no precedent and has had no sequel. There were as many in this year-and-a-half as in nearly the whole preceding, or the whole subsequent, decade. Most of the questions raised at most of these meetings went unresolved; many now seem irrelevant. But the first and last of these eleven meetings were noteworthy. The decisions taken at them were, in respect to the long-term interest of the Toronto faculty, disastrous. Their effects can still be felt.

Bissell had not intended to go to the meeting at which his formula for representation on a University Government Commission was to be presented for approval. He had taken its approval for granted, but "some vague forebodings" made him change his mind. He found the meeting, in the over-varnished, airless sterility of Cody Hall, hostile from the beginning. He described to the meeting his formula for representation: four faculty members, one of them an academic administrator; four students; two members of the Board of Governors;

one alumni member of the Senate. Anxious not to add to the Board's annoyance, he spoke dispassionately, without seeming to have a strong commitment to his proposal. Then two student leaders (both later to have national careers as NDP politicians) were invited to speak. These were Steven Langdon, President of the SAC, and Bob Rae. Though Rae's appeal was the more compelling, each made a clear, unequivocal plea for the disfranchisement on the proposed Commission of all but faculty and student members, on the simple grounds that staff and students constituted the University.

Jim Conacher, seconded by Howard Rapson, moved the adoption of Bissell's proposed formula. Kenneth McNaught then moved an amendment, that the two members of the Board of Governors be without the power to vote. McNaught, incidentally, had been Chairman of the Faculty Association at United College at the time of the Crowe case, and had been, along with Stewart Reid, one of the first to resign from the faculty in support of Crowe. After considerable debate, McNaught's amendment carried by a vote of 93 to 49. Bissell immediately left the meeting, which then went on to pass another amendment depriving the proposed alumni member of the Commission of the right to vote, and still another amendment to delete the requirement that one faculty member be an academic administrator. An amendment by Jack Robson, seconded by John Rist, to avoid staff-student equality on the Commission by raising the number of faculty representatives from four to five was defeated. The original motion, as amended, was then approved.

For some time after the October 3rd meeting Bissell contemplated resigning as President, thinking he had lost the confidence of the faculty. He may have been persuaded not to resign precipitately by a strong expression of support from senior faculty members in the days immediately following the meeting. Eventually he decided that the repudiation of his proposals at the meeting was unrepresentative of general faculty opinion. It is true that attendance at this meeting numbered only about 150, out of a faculty of 1,500, but there is little evidence that a larger meeting would have voted differently. As Bissell himself had noted, the composition, as well as the mood, of the faculty and of the faculty association was quite different in 1968 from that of a few years earlier. The cooperative faculty leaders interested in University government who had taken over direction of the faculty association in 1960 were now themselves becoming senior members of the staff, a little out of touch, some of them, with the outlook of many of the younger faculty members hired during the 1960s.

People like Larry Lynch, Brough Macpherson and Jim Conacher had come to the University before or shortly after the War, but half the faculty of 1968 had come, many of them straight out of American graduate schools, in the preceding half-dozen years. The University they had come to was, compared with the University before 1960, large, impersonal, chaotically expanding, often inefficiently administered. Salaries at Toronto in the 1960s had not kept up with those at many other North American universities, let alone those in other professions. Political divisions in society-at-large in the late 1960s were far sharper than they had been earlier, and, in contrast to most Toronto faculty in earlier times, many of the younger staff held political opinions firmly on the left. Some of them, at least, made little distinction between the University administration and the Board of Governors, seeing both as antagonists; and, for a moment, the notion of solidarity with student radicals was appealing.

The Board of Governors did not accept the legitimacy of the proposed Commission on University Government, regarding it only as a staff-student committee. Some Governors wished the Board to establish its own commission, but finally the Board simply stood somewhat sullenly aside and even agreed to appoint two members to serve as "observers" on the Commission. Staff and student members, four each, were duly elected to serve on the Commission, the faculty members by broad constituencies which ensured that two of the four came from the professional faculties. A result of the faculty electoral process was that only one member of the Commission, Larry Lynch, had had any experience in the faculty association's work for the reform of university government.

With Bissell as a voting member, the Commission began its work in January, 1969 and was to issue its Report in October. Although it received a number of briefs and presentations from the university community, the Commission did not arouse much faculty interest, and even less public interest. It worked in comparative isolation, its only "vital dialogue," Bissell wrote later, "between its own members." Ultimately the Commission on University Government did what committees frequently do when confronted with internal division and yet anxious to reach agreement. It made recommendations that effectively resolved its own internal tensions, but failed to take sufficient account of the world outside.

While the Commission was at work, the University climate was changing. Early in February the University of Toronto had its first brush with the uglier side of student radicalism, when Clark Kerr, who had been President at Berkeley, was abusively interrupted and harassed during a speech which he was able to finish only by allowing a rebuttal by several members of the New Left Caucus. In the calendar of radical student violence in the late 1960s the Clark Kerr incident was trivial, but it was the first clear evidence at Toronto of the willingness of "revolutionary" student leaders to threaten violence. Bissell later wrote of the "ugly genie of hate" that had suddenly filled the room where Kerr spoke.

Later in the year a determined handful of student zealots disrupted the annual dinner for University College freshmen, and in September organized a somewhat incoherent teach-in that disrupted some other University functions. In the wider world, violence in the universities was constantly in the news, even in Canada. Student protesters at Sir George Williams whom police had attempted to eject during a sit-in had wrecked computer installations, destroyed records and damaged other University property. In April, the administration building at Harvard was occupied by protesters, some of whom were injured by the police attack that cleared the building. And at Cornell black activists seized the students' union and were eventually shown on the continent's television screens filing out in improvised uniforms, some carrying rifles.

Among the many decayed institutions at Toronto was the University disciplinary body, the Caput, composed of senior administrators and long disused. Bissell had established a committee chaired by Ralph Campbell, an agricultural economist, later to be President of the University of Manitoba, to recommend new disciplinary procedures; the Campbell Report when it was released early in the fall was vague, confused, and placatory on the subject of disruptions and demonstrations, and alarmed rather than reassured faculty members and others concerned about peace and order on campus.

As the language of the radical student leaders became more aggressive and rigid in its conventions, the momentary feelings of solidarity which many merely liberal faculty members had entertained towards student activists took flight. The few faculty members who joined in the shrill, or sour, or heavy Marxist sloganeering of the student left contributed to the growing hostility of most of their colleagues to student demands. Later it became clear that what was happening was only a mild and local reflection of a massive reaction against student revolutionists all over the western world. Indeed, the far left was about to be driven from the field in the wider society as well.

The Report of the Commission on University Government was released early in October, 1969. It was the result of nearly eight months of, sometimes, intense work. It was written almost entirely by Bob Rae and Larry Lynch, who had also dominated the Commission's deliberations. Bissell, still stung by the student-faculty rejection of his formula for representation, took little part in discussion, though he signed the Report. The Report, especially in its introduction and conclusion, was well-written, even thoughtful. Given its premises, it made symmetrical sense. The trouble was that its basic premise, that faculty and students should share an equal responsibility for making academic decisions, was wrong.

The faculty association was now faced with the, perhaps, predictable consequences of its casual enthusiasm for staff-student solidarity the year before. Since none of the faculty members on the CUG had consulted with the ATS, the Report came as a surprise. It recommended as a unitary top governing structure for the University (the Commission had not seriously discussed reforming the Board of Governors and the Senate), a Governing Council made up of equal numbers of faculty, student, and lay members—twenty of each with an additional six academic administrators. The principle of staff-student parity was recommended as a model for the reform of inferior bodies throughout the University—faculty and departmental councils. Students were also to have a voice equal to faculty in matters of faculty appointment, promotion, dismissal, and tenure. Here, ostensibly in order to allay faculty fears, final recommendations were to be made solely by departmental chairmen. This embodied what Bissell called the principle of "complex parity"—decisive mediation by academic administrators in cases of faculty-student conflict.

The general faculty reaction to the CUG Report's recommendations was much more hostile than welcoming. While initially there may have been a degree of faculty indifference to the proposal for staff-student parity in the top governing body, resistance to "parity" strengthened when it came to faculty and departmental councils, and most faculty members found the recommendations regarding appointments, promotions, and dismissals unacceptable. There was, to be sure, some faculty support for the CUG recommendations among people who either trusted academic administrators to side with faculty members, or, in the case of a few, believed still in the promise of staff-student cooperation.

It was the CUG Report that led to my first involvement in the faculty association. I had not even been a member of the ATS, having had no interest in a faculty role in governing the University, the issue that seemed to dominate the Association's activities during the 1960s. But I did take an active part, first in the History Department's resistance to the CUG recommendations for staff-student parity in departmental affairs, and then in the fight over the Report that took place in the Council of the Faculty of Arts and Science. Some colleagues in the Political Economy Department, particularly Steve Dupré and Art Kruger, had brought several of us together to plan a response in the Faculty Council to the CUG recommendations. John Rist, from the Classics Department, and I agreed to present a number of motions to the Council rejecting staff-student parity.

Rist was a somewhat combative Englishman notably lacking in deference towards the University administration. It may be that he from a British background and I from an American, found it easier than some of our Canadian colleagues whose whole careers had been at Toronto to oppose forthrightly the temporizing measures of the University administration towards student demands. In any event, Rist and I worked closely together through a series of meetings of the Arts and Science Council where staff-student equality in academic decision-making was debated. Eventually the Council passed our motions rejecting a student voice in matters of faculty appointment, promotion, tenure, and dismissal, and also rejecting staff-student parity on the governing bodies of faculties, departments, and colleges. Some of the meetings where these matters were discussed were lively, even exciting. For a time in the winter of 1969-70 the Arts and Science Council was the central focus for debate on the University's future, its meetings eagerly awaited, attended by hundreds of faculty and students, full of noise and occasionally passion. Once the question of its composition was settled, the Council lapsed into a torpor from which it has never awakened.

The character of the faculty response at Toronto to proposals for staff-student equality in academic decision-making was more complex than many people at the time supposed. Virtually all the student leaders, most of the academic administrators, and many ordinary faculty members saw the issue simply in terms of right and left—conservatives and reactionaries opposed to a substantial student role; liberals and radicals supportive towards it.

This view of the division of faculty opinion was true for some. There were a good many conservative faculty members flatly opposed to a student role in deciding academic matters, and there was a much smaller group in favour. But there were many whose view of this question was entwined with their view of the University administration. Most faculty administrators, some would-be administrators, some conservatives who still trusted the administration, were able to persuade themselves that administrative mediation could neutralize any threat of real student power. On the other hand, a number of us objected to the proposed new role for students precisely because of the power it implicitly assigned to the administration. The recommendations of the CUG Report seemed to offer a sinister prospect of administrators using students to neutralize any independent faculty influence in University affairs.

Because the various shades of faculty opinion were not always obvious at the time, it was easy to make mistakes in appraising others. I can recall being both irritated and amused by the, no doubt, well-intended efforts some University administrators made to reassure us about student power by pointing out that they, the administrators, would hold the real and final power. It was hard to tell them that this was exactly what concerned us.

At the time, in the fall of 1969, that Rist and I were dealing with the CUG recommendations in the Arts and Science Faculty Council,

Rist was elected Chairman of the ATS for the coming year. He persuaded me to chair the ATS University Government Committee and help shape an ATS response to the CUG Report. Our committee held a dozen meetings during the winter of 1969-70. We considered the evolving forms of university government at a number of Canadian and American universities. We received some written submissions, and met with a number of interested Toronto faculty members. Unlike the CUG Commission, we seriously considered recommending a reformed bicameral government for the University. It was clear that the most effective governing structures at other North American universities combined a lay, or mainly lay, board with a strong faculty-dominated senate with financial as well as academic responsibilities. John Crispo spoke to us persuasively in advocating a reformed Board of Governors and Senate linked by a joint committee that would deal with both academic and financial proposals.

While we were at work, Bissell was pressing ahead with a plan to achieve University consensus on a unicameral governing structure. He set up a CUG Programming Committee smoothly chaired by Marty Friedland of the Law Faculty which organized plans for a kind of constitutional convention—a University-Wide Committee to meet at the end of the academic year and try to reach agreement on a scheme for the governance of the University that could be taken to the provincial government as an expression of the University's common will. Our committee and the ATS Council were apprehensive about the proposal for a University-Wide Committee, fearing it would be dominated by administrators and students. We wanted the faculty association not to take part in the University-Wide Committee, but to make a separate submission to the provincial government, but we were overruled at an ill-attended general meeting of the ATS on a motion by Howard Rapson.

What might be taken as the University administration's view of the most acceptable formula for us to propose for representation on a unicameral governing body was laid out in a plan brought to our committee by Brough Macpherson. This scheme would have retained a unicameral governing council of sixty-six members, as in the CUG Report, but would have reduced student membership slightly, from twenty to eighteen, and increased faculty representation sharply, from twenty to thirty-three—half the total membership. This increase would have been largely at the expense of the lay component which would have shrunk from twenty to nine. Of all the numerical solutions proposed to the question of faculty-student-lay representation on a governing body, those in the Macpherson proposal were the most unrealistic. Perhaps, whether consciously or not, they were brought to us partly to try to divert us from repudiating unicameralism altogether. As well, of course, Macpherson had for years advocated a major role for faculty in university government.

The faculty people involved in the 1960s in the reform of university government were now going off in different directions. Macpherson had retained a kind of innocent and good-natured faith in both the faculty and the administration. Larry Lynch, of course, was committed to the CUG proposals and was surprised and perhaps a little embittered at the vehemence of faculty opposition to them. Bob Greene was steering a judicious course sympathetic in measured degree to students, faculty, and administration. Only Jim Conacher had firmly aligned himself with faculty opponents of the CUG Report. While I did not distrust Macpherson himself, I was uneasy about the views of some of those who supported his proposal. It was signed by Bert Allen, the Dean of Arts and Science, by Bob Greene who was to be his successor, and by, among a few others, two future presidents of the University, Jim Ham and George Connell, as well as by Howard Rapson.

On our little university government committee we had a political problem and, perhaps, a moral dilemma as well. Years later Art Kruger, who was a member of the committee, was to remind me that, at one point, we discovered that a majority of us on the committee really favoured a reformed bicameral governing structure for the University. To have proposed this, however, would not only have brought us into direct conflict with the administration, but would have sharply divided the faculty association. While support for a faculty-student alliance had faded fast among the faculty, there was still strong support for a unicameral governing structure. Nothing had changed the faculty's view of the irrelevance of the Board of Governors and the University Senate. In many ways, it would have been easier, of course, to have reformed both bodies than to have attempted to create a completely new governing structure. But it was clear to us that if we opted for a reformed bicameral government we would split the faculty association and might very well be defeated as well. So we tried to make the best of unicameralism.

We proposed a governing council made up of twenty faculty members, twenty laymen, eight administrators and seven students. The faculty association accepted our general arguments, but eventually raised the proposed numbers of students and administrators to ten each. We took this formula to the meetings of the University-Wide Committee, held on the first three days of June, 1970. After a good deal of numerical legerdemain, this body agreed on a unicameral governing structure something like that which we had proposed, but with the student component raised to two-thirds that of the faculty. The faculty association endorsed the University-Wide Committee's recommendations and, for a moment, there was an optimistic assumption that the University had successfully come to agreement on a workable plan for reform.

It was a year before the provincial government got around to legislating a new Governing Act for the University. For part of that time, Bill Davis, first as Minister of University Affairs and then as Premier, was considering whether or not to endorse the unicameral principle. He conscientiously canvassed opinions. In November,

1970, very shortly before he moved up to the premiership, he and his deputy met with John Rist and me. Davis asked us a good many questions, most insistently whether a unicameral system of university government would really work. I told him, wrongly I now think, that it could not be worse than what we had.

By the spring of 1971, Davis had decided to bring in a unicameral governing act, but with one condition that substantially changed what all our various university schemes had proposed. That was simply, as might have been predicted, to insist on a lay component amounting to half the membership of a new governing body. The first reading of the new Act was in early June. It preserved the recommendations of the University-Wide Committee except for sharply increasing the lay component and sensibly reducing the total membership of the new Governing Council to fifty from the seventy-two proposed by that Committee.

There was a final encounter with student radicals in the legislative hearings that followed first reading of the new Act. They once again raised the issue of staff-student parity. I was out of the country that summer, but a number of faculty association leaders took a vigorous part in these hearings. For these colleagues—Jim Conacher, Ron Missen, Charles Hanly, Jack Robson, Art Kruger, John Rist, and Stan Schiff—the hostility of many members of the provincial legislature towards the faculty at the University was startling. Opposition members from the Liberal and NDP parties engaged in ostentatious populist posturing in their support of student protests at "faculty arrogance." Perhaps partly with a view to forthcoming elections in which eighteen-year-olds would have the vote, some of the Tory members joined in professor-bashing. The Minister of University Affairs, John White, leaned towards supporting an amendment which would have, in effect, given students a membership equal to faculty on the new governing body of the University. White, incidentally, is perhaps best remembered at the University for his memorable observation that what Ontario needed from its universities was "more scholars for the dollar."

In the end, faced with opposition to staff-student parity from the Toronto newspapers and, more crucially, with a last-minute intervention from Claude Bissell, Premier Davis and thus the legislature, stayed with the formula of the University-Wide Committee in respect to staff-student numbers. The new Governing Act replaced the old Board of Governors and Senate with a Governing Council of fifty members: twenty-four laymen (of whom eight were to be elected alumni); twelve elected faculty members; eight elected student members; and six administrators including the President and Chancellor.

Writing a year or two after the governing Act of 1971 was passed, and still in a spirit of some optimism, Bissell complimented the faculty association for having produced "the most compelling statement ... and ... the best specific proposal" for the reform of university government at Toronto. He was referring to our committee's recommendations which I wrote, and which still seem to me to have a certain plausibility. Our basic argument was that the indivisibility of the University's social, academic, and financial needs implied unified direction by a body widely representative of both the University and general public. We went on to justify a major lay component in such a body, but also to argue for an internal majority of members from the University. Bissell concluded that while Davis's decision sharply to increase the lay representation deprived the new Governing Council of an internal majority, the eight alumni members would have close university associations and could be regarded as nearly internal.

Bissell's optimism was not to be justified by subsequent developments. Almost immediately the new Governing Council showed signs of fatal weakness. It continued for years to fret over the relative importance of the various "estates" represented on it. It made a crucial early decision that none of its committees would have a majority from any one "estate." This meant that the Academic Affairs Committee would have only a minority of faculty members, and there were to be occasions when an academic decision was taken by a majority of the Committee with all the faculty members opposed. Worse, the Governing Council as a whole proved utterly unable to deliberate thoughtfully, to initiate policies, or to challenge the administration. Within a few years, it had become essentially a rubber stamp for the University administration, leavening its helplessness with occasional rhetorical and petulant assertions of self-importance.

Both contributing to and arising from its weakness was the persistent mediocrity of the Governing Council's membership. While there were certainly, over the years, numerous individual members— students, faculty, and laymen—who, against considerable odds, showed energy, intelligence, and efficiency, there was a persistent majority of dull, or uninformed, or apathetic members. The kind of laymen from the established business elite of Toronto who had frequently served on the old Board of Governors were rarely persuaded to serve without power or prestige on the new Council. Whatever flicker of tentative goodwill the faculty might have entertained towards the new body at the beginning was shortly extinguished by the hostility towards professors regularly shown by student and lay members, and the faculty simply lost interest in the Governing Council. It also proved impossible to arouse any serious interest in the Governing Council among students-at-large. It was sometimes difficult to fill student vacancies, and the student-politicians who did serve often did so merely to polish their public skills and acquire credentials for a career in law or business. In short, the Toronto experiment in unitary government was to be an anachronism from the day of its birth, a feeble memorial to an imperfect vision of university autonomy from the 1960s.

Why did this Toronto experiment work so badly? One reason was a fundamental flaw in representation on the Governing Council. All the university proposals for such a body, however much they differed in other respects, had foreseen a faculty component of at least a third of the total membership, and also a majority of members from within the university community. As defined by the Act of 1971, however, faculty membership was less than one-quarter of the whole, and there was a lay majority. Bissell's wistful assumption that the alumni members would be virtually "internal" in their outlook was unjustified. More serious was a basic misconception about student members that almost all of us had shared. Once the impulse of student radicalism had faded, the student members of the Governing Council behaved like the lay members. They retained a few ritualized slogans in support of student interests, but in most respects they were ignorant of academic matters, conservative in fiscal matters, and deferential to the University administration. In dealing with most University issues, they were simply part of the lay majority.

The Governing Council, in short, was not a unitary body combining a capacity for making intelligent academic decisions with expertise in dealing with financial questions. It was, rather, a weakened, diluted, cumbersome Board of Governors. But if the Board of Governors had survived, however mutilated, in the new body, the old Senate had disappeared entirely, and Toronto was left the only major university in the English-speaking world in which the faculty had no dominant voice in making purely academic decisions.

Given the weakness of the governing body defined by the Act of 1971, it is no surprise that the real power in the management of the University's resources rapidly passed into the hands of the University administration. The casually assembled advisory committees that Bissell had used in the 1960s were institutionalized in the 1970s as part of the University administration and without the kind of regular faculty consultation that had been part of Bissell's procedures. The faculty association, which in the middle 1960s had seen itself as central to the governance of the University, and which had, for a decade, sought and expected a major role in the reformation of the University, was left with little. Indeed, except for the augmented role faculty now had under the Haist Rules in making academic appointments, faculty influence in the management of the University was clearly less than it had been before 1960.

Looking back now at the faculty preoccupation with university government in the 1960s, one can see in it a curious mixture of good intentions and selflessness, combined with arrogance and self-deception. The reform of university government was a preoccupation, incidentally, nearly universal in Canadian universities, though given, perhaps, a special intensity at Toronto because of the sympathetic leadership of President Bissell. A primary attraction of a decisive faculty role in university government was, of course, that it seemed to resolve the uneasy tension between the professional self-esteem that faculty members felt and their formal position as mere university employees. The dread of seeing themselves only as employees of the University was entrenched at Toronto, at least among senior faculty. The notion of faculty power, of a faculty-run university, was so appealing that it became, for a time, almost a matter of faith. It seems now, in its shallowness and evasion of reality, a little like the easy old socialist assumption that nationalization of industry led inevitably to socialization.

In fact, universities were becoming inevitably more rigidly bureaucratic in their management as well as ever more constrained by the mechanical formulas of government funding. Let us, for the sake of argument, suppose that the issue of student power had never arisen in the late 1960s and that, in some form or other, the Toronto faculty association had gained a primary place in the government of the University. In earlier times, before the expansion of the 1960s, such a development might have given faculty a substantial degree of control over their University environment. But, given the bureaucratic structure of the new University, it would merely have ensured that a little group of anointed faculty governors became a part of management. This would have weakened, rather than strengthened, independent faculty influence in University affairs. It may well have been a blessing that the drive for faculty power in the 1960s came to nothing.

Chapter Four
Collective Bargaining—
The First Attempt

While university government was the focus of the faculty association's activities during the 1960s, the association did carry on its salary and benefits work. The question of pensions was a special, though often frustrating, concern of the ATS in these years. The Pension Committee was one of four standing committees of the association, along with the Salary, Policy, and University Government Committees. Faculty pensions at Toronto, as at most universities, had a somewhat tortuous history. Before 1929 the only pensions available were the Carnegie Allowances, funded originally by Andrew Carnegie to provide relief from penury to retired professors at North American universities. These were non-contributory pensions which, in earlier years, had paid eligible recipients an annual stipend of $1000.

In 1929 the Carnegie Foundation stopped making new grants and set a maximum of $1500 as an annual payment for remaining recipients. The TIAA, or TI&AA as it was originally called (Teachers' Insurance and Annuity Association) was promptly expanded in the United States to take the place of the Carnegie grants, and Toronto had a TIAA plan from 1929 to 1945. Because of wartime exchange restrictions combined with a trace of patriotism, the TIAA connection was severed in 1945, and a similar plan undertaken through the Canada Life Assurance Company.

The two principal types of University pensions are, of course, money purchase plans and defined benefit plans. Both the TIAA and Canada Life plans at Toronto were money purchase plans based on an annual investment of 10% of a participant's salary (5% from the participant and 5% from the University). The funds thus accrued then became available at retirement to finance a participant's pension. The advantages of money-purchase plans lay in their potential equity growth, depending, of course, on how the funds were invested, as well as their simplicity and portability. Their disadvantage lay in the risk of market fluctuations and, if funds were conservatively invested, their erosion by inflation. A few retired Toronto professors are still drawing pensions from these old plans, a handful, indeed, from the pre-war TIAA plan. The old TIAA plan did not, incidentally, have the stock purchase option added later under CREF (College Retirement Equities Fund) and, having been funded from contributions from pre-inflation salaries, provided tiny benefits.

In 1955 the Board of Governors adopted a new and, as it turned out, unsatisfactory pension plan. This was a defined benefit plan, but one based on earnings averaged over a participant's entire University career—a so-called career average, or unit purchase plan. It paid an annual pension amounting to 2% of average annual earnings times a member's years of service. With absolutely stable salaries, it would have paid, for a member with thirty-five years' service, about half his final salary. But such a plan took no account of inflation, with the result that faculty members retiring in the late 1950s with final salaries of about $10,000 were receiving pensions of $2,000 to $2,500 per year. The ATS Pension Committee reported in 1958 that at McGill a defined benefits plan based on 1/60th final average earnings over the last five years times years of service was paying members who retired at $10,000 salaries, $5,000, or more than twice that of the Toronto plan. For several years the McGill plan was regularly cited by the Toronto Pension Committee as a model.

The Finance Committee of the Board of Governors considered submissions from the ATS Pension Committee and studied the McGill plan, as well as final average earning plans then being implemented in the provincial and federal civil service, and for Ontario teachers. There is no clear evidence, however, that the Board paid much more attention to the faculty association's pension complaints than it did to salary complaints. In 1961 the Board did supplement the 1955 plan with a complex formula that related it to a final average earnings plan, and brought the Toronto plan about half-way to the McGill plan. By 1963 the Board was committed to a final average earnings plan, but it did not come fully into place until 1966. This was the genesis of the present Toronto pension plan and initially paid 1 1/2% of the average salary over the last five years times years of service, or 40-50% of final salary to members whose whole career had been at Toronto.

One consequence of the complicated succession and overlapping of pension plans was that it was difficult, for a number of years, to calculate definitely what a retiring professor's pension should be. The University office that administered pensions was inefficient, confused, and often insensitive. There were a number of complaints like that of a retiring professor of chemistry who, in 1966, told the ATS that he had not even received a reply to his repeated requests for an estimate of what pension he would receive. Women, as mentioned earlier, fared even worse than men, receiving in the early 1960s pensions averaging about 30% of final salaries, while retiring men were receiving about 40% of salaries that were themselves 50% above those of women.

If the success of the ATS pension committees in influencing the Board of Governors was problematic, they did offer a basic education on pensions to ATS members, as well as give useful support to individual members in their pension dealings with the University. A number of people in the ATS acted as volunteer pension counsellors. Don

Baillie deserves special mention. An actuarial scientist in the Mathematics Department, he chaired and served on a succession of ATS pension committees, and advised retiring members on pension matters for more than a generation until well past his own retirement. For a number of years in the early 1970s, Charles Hebdon spent his own retirement in a little office in the OCUFA headquarters giving clearminded advice on pension and tax matters to Toronto and other faculty members. Not infrequently Hebdon was able to obtain a substantial increase in pensions offered to retiring professors who sought his help. This, of course, raised an uneasy question about the pension settlements accepted by those who did not complain.

In dealing with the question of pensions, the faculty association suffered essentially the same weakness that hindered its salary and other benefit requests. It could not negotiate, but only ask. The Board of Governors made its own arrangements, taking into account what was happening in other universities, elsewhere in the public service, and, occasionally, even in private business. Nor was the Board always free of self-interest. Several members of the Board had connections with Canada Life when the Toronto plan was transferred to it from TIAA. In one respect, however, Toronto faculty profited from the non-university outlook of the Board. University pensions did not generally provide widows' benefits, but the pension plans in the chartered banks did, and it was on the recommendation of banker members of the Board of Governors that the Toronto plan included provision for widows.

By 1962, faculty discontent with salaries was rising sharply in Toronto. The salary settlement for 1962-63, an average rise of 2.5%, was the poorest for a number of years. The average salary at Toronto in 1962-63 was $9362, about the same as at Queen's and McGill, but below that at Alberta and well below that at Laval. Average salaries at major American universities were 10-20% higher. Perhaps remembering the meeting arranged by Sidney Smith in 1951, Bora Laskin, then

ATS Chairman, proposed to Bissell a meeting of the ATS Executive with members of the Board of Governors to discuss salary. Bissell's reply was bluntly discouraging: the Board of Governors, he said, did not want to meet with faculty association representatives, did not want to "negotiate" with faculty. Bissell went on to question the legitimacy of the ATS in speaking for the faculty, since only 60% were ATS members. Besides, he told Laskin, heads, deans, and directors could also serve as a "legitimate source of information" for the Board. "I know," Bissell concluded, "that you are as keenly aware as I am of the dangers of creating an employer-employee atmosphere."

Later in the fall of 1962 Bissell wrote Laskin that the University could not accede to faculty association demands for a rise in salary floors, that he wanted to raise salary *averages* rather than floors, to reward merit rather than make across-the-board increases. Merit awards, rather than across-the-board increases, Bissell concluded, "allows flexibility and judgment." This was to be a persistent theme in the University administration's statements on salaries for years to come. Bissell did, shortly after this, attempt to reassure the faculty association about long-term salary prospects. The Board of Governors, he reported, intended (l) that faculty salaries would rise "for a number of years"; (2) that Toronto salaries should be the highest in Canada and competitive with those at most of the senior American universities; and (3) that there would, from time-to-time, be a raise in salary scales, though "merit" would remain the primary criterion for increases.

The rapid, if abortive, advance in faculty involvement in university government in the mid-1960s did appear, for a time, to open up a new avenue of faculty association influence in salary determinations. In the fall of 1965 Howard Rapson, then chairing the Salary committee, reported that there were three ATS representatives serving, for the first time, on a committee on salaries of University administrators and members of the Board of Governors. There was considerable anticipation at that time of a substantial salary increase, perhaps 15%. In the event, the salary settlement for 1966-67 provided for an average increase of 9%.

The ATS was concerned for a number of years in the 1960s with problems of its membership, these given point by Bissell's doubts in 1962 about the Association's claim to represent the faculty. In earlier times members had rejoined annually by paying their dues. In 1963 the University began deducting dues from salary for those members who requested it. Many members, however, did not rejoin the Association after returning from leave, and, more important, many of the new faculty members being appointed in record numbers did not join at all.

In 1965, after a poll of members strongly endorsed it, an "opt-out" scheme of membership and dues collection was adopted by which existing as well as new members of the teaching staff became ATS members and had their dues deducted by the University administration unless they resigned from the Association. This measure effectively reversed the decline in membership as a proportion of total faculty and, by the end of the decade, the Association's membership was fairly stable at about two-thirds of its potential. Dues, incidentally, continued to rise, though remaining very low by subsequent standards—rising from $9/year in 1960 to $30/year in 1968, of which most went to CAUT and, from 1967 on, to OCUFA as well.

Despite Bissell's assurances, Toronto salaries lagged in the 1960s relative to those at other Canadian and American universities and, especially, relative to salaries in the public service and among private professional people. In 1964 an ATS study disclosed that average Toronto salaries had fallen below those at Queen's and McGill as well as below those at Laval and Alberta. Toronto appeared even worse off when average salaries were related to the age of faculty members. For example, in 1964 the average salary for full professors at Toronto was below that at York though the average full professor at Toronto was

Collective Bargaining—The First Attempt

seven years older than his counterpart at York. The average salary for assistant professors at Toronto was below that at seven other Canadian universities and the average age of such people at Toronto was above that of all but one of these seven. The average age of lecturers at Toronto was higher than at any of the other universities studied and the average salary lower than at fifteen others.

Looked at superficially, Toronto salary increases in the 1960s do not seem to have been so bad. There were, for example, average increases of 9% in 1966-67 and 10% in 1967-68. Taking the decade as a whole, salary increases averaged about 7% a year, this at a time when the annual rate of inflation until near the end of the decade averaged not much above 2% a year. This apparent gain over the rate of inflation seems to have been in sharp contrast to the substantial fall in real wages in the decade after the War, or in the 1970s to follow.

But the 7% annual increase in these years was a raw average. It concealed what, for a large new faculty in its most productive years, would later be separately identified as a progress-through-the-ranks (PTR) component, that is, a component representing the normal career progress of faculty members as they rose in rank. This component, if separately identified in the 1960s, would have probably been closer to 4% than 3% annually. If it is added to the 2% inflation rate, the real increase in average salaries was probably only one or two per cent a year. And this itself reflected large merit increases paid to relatively few faculty members, rather than across-the-board increases, since salary floors were raised only once during the decade, by a flat $1000 for all ranks.

By the late 1960s the cost of living in Toronto was rising much more rapidly than in Canada as a whole, although it was rising nationally as well. In 1968-69 the CPI was up to an annual rate of 4.5% and the Toronto salary settlement was 5.4%. The cost of housing, in particular, had become a major problem for young Toronto faculty members. The average house price in Toronto in the mid-1950s had been about $15,000; by the mid-1960s it was still only $16,000; by early 1969 it was $28,000, having achieved only the first of four doublings it was to go through in the next two decades. In the meantime, the income of other professionals had risen much higher than that of university faculty, and, indeed, so had the income of others in the work force. In 1969 the electricians, plumbers, and sheet metal workers employed at the University of Toronto were paid an average annual wage of about $13,000—almost exactly the same as the average assistant professor, and the wages of these workers had risen about 20% in the preceding year.

By 1969 there was growing faculty resentment not merely at inadequate salary settlements, but at the absence of real salary negotiations with the administration. In February the ATS Council passed a motion asking either for direct salary negotiations with the provincial government or negotiations with the Board of Governors, followed, if necessary, by mediation "and ultimately arbitration." The Salary and Benefits Committee appointed in the fall of 1969 was dominated, for the first time, by young members from Arts departments, people who had come to the University in the 1960s. The new Salary and Benefits chairman was Wayne Sumner from the Philosophy Department, far more militant than his predecessors.

Sumner sent ATS members a stream of information about the relative decline of Toronto salaries since 1960 when Toronto had had the highest salary floors and highest salary averages by rank in Canada. Now, in 1969, Toronto salaries were not only falling behind those at a number of other Canadian universities, but had declined even more dramatically in comparison with those in the provincial and federal civil service, those of secondary school teachers, and, of course, those of other professional people. Average faculty salaries at the University were now less than half those of doctors, lawyers, engineers and architects. Writing of a mood in the faculty association "more militant than at any time in recent years," Sumner said the explanation for this was simply that "something had gone very seriously wrong both with academic salaries in general and with salaries at the university in particular."

An ATS General Meeting approved Sumner's demand for formal negotiation of salary and benefits including binding arbitration if necessary. This demand was subsequently endorsed in a mail ballot to members by a vote of 471 to 32. Under increasing pressure, Bissell and the University Budget Committee (on which there now sat three elected faculty members) agreed to meet with the ATS Salary Committee.

Discussions with the Budget Committee were civil to begin with, and the Budget Committee did agree to provide the faculty association with some information which had previously been withheld, such as salary averages by rank and division and preliminary budgetary estimates. But in a meeting on February 18, 1970, the Budget Committee flatly refused to "negotiate" with the ATS or discuss any form of impasse resolution. After this meeting Sumner told the ATS membership that the Budget Committee was apparently thinking of a six per cent salary increase for 1970-71. Bissell bitterly protested this inference, called it "astounding," and accused Sumner of presenting an "inaccurate and misleading picture" of the meeting. At another meeting with the Budget Committee a week later Sumner and his colleagues made their case for a 16% salary increase, were listened to in silence, and not invited for further discussion. The Budget Committee recommended a 9% average increase, and this was eventually announced to Deans and Directors, not to the faculty association.

Believing he had a mandate from the overwhelming support he had received in his poll of the faculty, Sumner asked the ATS Council to approve a motion asking faculty members to resign from the Budget Committee, and a second motion censuring the Budget Committee for refusing to meet with the ATS Salary Committee. There was some opposition to this in the Council from conservatives in the

professional faculties, notably from Michael Uzumeri, a civil engineer, and Kent Barker from the School of Architecture, but the Council passed Sumner's motions handily, and put the question of salary
negotiations at the top of the agenda for the Annual Meeting of the
faculty association on March 30th. Sumner tried to assure faculty
support for his negotiating demands by sending out a detailed newsletter to the whole ATS membership.

While there was clearly strong support for Sumner from most Arts
faculty, there was considerable opposition to his demand for real
collective bargaining from some of the professional faculties, notably
from the powerful Engineering faculty, and, as well, from some of the
Science departments in Arts and Science. Indeed, on this issue there
was to be tension within the faculty for some years, with Engineering
members, notably Uzumeri, Ben Etkin, and Howard Rapson, leading
the attack on what seemed to them to be trade union tactics. Many
younger Arts faculty saw these people as reactionaries, obsequious to
the administration, and indifferent to the plight of faculty members
without major grants or outside income. They, on the other hand, saw
themselves as maintaining the traditional role of university faculty,
and saw their critics on the Arts faculty as mere schoolteachers, attracted to collective bargaining tactics because of their own professional insecurity.

As good a case as could be made against formal collective bargaining was made by Howard Rapson in a paper he wrote on the subject
at this time. Rapson raised several serious objections to collective
bargaining and binding arbitration. First, he pointed out that the
University's income was based on enrollment formulas provided by
the government of Ontario and that no form of bargaining within the
University could increase these funds. Effective bargaining would
have to be carried on directly with the provincial government. If not,
any settlement favourable to the faculty would have to be made at the

expense of other University needs—support staff, new academic appointments, books and laboratory equipment, and maintenance.

Second, he noted the faculty association's support for a form of government in the University "in which the dominant role will be played by the academic staff." If this ambition succeeded, as then still seemed likely, faculty collective bargaining would mean that academic staff would be negotiating salary increases with other academic staff, an indefensible prospect. Finally, as to arbitration, Rapson argued that it would be irresponsible to turn over to outside arbitrators the major decisions regarding the academic life of the University, since faculty salaries represented nearly half the total budget. Most of Rapson's arguments were to be echoed tirelessly by the University administration for many years to come. Some are still to be heard.

The Annual Meeting on March 30, 1970 was the eleventh general meeting of the faculty association in a year-and-a-half. For two entire academic years there had been a general meeting every few weeks. Predictably, members were getting tired of meetings, and attendance had been dwindling. At the Meeting of March 2nd, Rapson, likeminded colleagues, and supporters of the University administration had discovered how easy it was, at an ill-attended meeting, to defeat proposals approved by the ATS Executive and Council. This was when our attempt to prevent the ATS from taking part in the University-Wide Committee was thwarted by a motion of Rapson's. The Annual Meeting, of course, with Sumner's negotiating proposals before it, was likely to be much better-attended. But Rapson, supported by his fellow faculty members on the Budget Committee, Bob Greene and Tim Rooney, decided to challenge Sumner's collective bargaining proposals directly.

It became apparent as members assembled for the evening meeting on March 30th that this was not the usual ATS crowd. There was a group of regular attenders; there were also a number of irregular attenders, mainly from Arts departments, there to support Sumner;

but there were many more engineers than usual, as well as a good many people from other conservative professional faculties who were not usually active in faculty association affairs. I recall, in particular, a group of women wearing hats and sitting together who, it was said, were from the Nursing Faculty.

Sumner put a three-part motion before the meeting: first, to censure the University administration for refusing to negotiate salaries; second, to censure the Budget Committee for refusing to meet with the ATS Salary Committee; and third, to call on the faculty members of the Budget Committee, Rapson, Greene, and Rooney, to resign from the Committee. After lively debate, the question was put on the first part of the motion. It was defeated by a vote of 107 to 74. Sumner withdrew the remainder of his motion and resigned as Chairman of the Salary Committee. The other members of the Committee present also resigned.

When the Chairman, John Rist, asked the meeting for further advice, Charles Hanly, hoping to limit the damage, moved simply that the meeting reaffirm the faculty association's salary policy. This motion too was defeated, though by a narrower margin than Sumner's. Eventually the meeting finished its other business and adjourned, the faculty association's first serious attempt at collective bargaining shattered. Claude Bissell later recalled the faculty association's repudiation of its own salary policy as one of the events in March of 1970 that allowed him to "feel relieved and moderately cheerful."

The effects of the Annual Meeting of March, 1970 on faculty interests at the University of Toronto were as drastic, if not as long-lasting, as the disastrous effects of the faculty association's endorsement of staff-student parity on the Commission to examine university government in October, 1968. For the next few years the University administration paid very little attention to the faculty association's salary submissions. Indeed, in 1970-71 the association did not even have a proper salary committee. No one could be found to

chair such a committee in the fall of 1970, so an improvised committee was struck.

We who were on this committee sensibly avoided any discussion
of collective bargaining when we met with the Budget Committee
and, instead, made the best argument we could for a clear separation
of across-the-board from merit increases, and for the need to remove
decisions on merit increases from the unaccountable hands of deans
and directors. We were listened to, but no action was taken on our
proposals and the Budget Committee refused further meetings. Our
proposals were, however, the genesis of a distinction between components of salary increases that the association was to pursue vigorously
and that Michael Finlayson was to develop into the progress-through-
the ranks formula a couple of years later.

For twenty years the faculty association's main concerns had been
to influence salary settlements and gain a place of real influence in the
government of the University. By 1971 it was clear that both these
efforts had failed. The disillusionment of many Toronto faculty members was palpable. Association membership declined ten per cent in
1971, and attendance at (now infrequent) general meetings fell. Yet,
as an organization, the faculty association carried on busily as if nothing had happened. Indeed, the present University of Toronto Faculty
Association (UTFA) came into being on the first of July, 1971 after
the constitution had been changed in order to change the name,
change the title of the old "Chairman" to "President," and change
slightly the composition of the Council. A new formula provided
representation on the Council to the then new colleges—New, Erin-
dale, and Scarborough—but left the smaller professional schools
heavily over-represented. The professional faculties were given three-
fifths of the seats on the new Council, though their membership was
less than half the Association total.

The change in the name of the organization from "Association of
the Teaching Staff" to "Faculty Association" had been proposed to a

general meeting as early as 1964 by the Policy Committee; at that time, "no strong feeling was expressed, and the matter was referred to Council" where it died. Many older members, in fact, disliked the term "faculty" for members of the teaching staff, regarding it as an Americanism, and preferring to keep "faculty" as a designation for units of the University, such as the "Faculty of Arts and Science." By 1971 this no longer seemed to be an issue.

Although the new Governing Act of 1971 destroyed any real prospect of the faculty association having significant influence on the government of the University, this was not immediately obvious to everyone. There were at least two echoes of earlier battles. One was the formation in September, 1971 of the Faculty Reform Caucus, aimed at giving a voice within the faculty association to those members who still supported a student-faculty alliance and wished to counter what they perceived as the reactionary self-interest of those now dominating UTFA. Among the founders of the Caucus were Wayne Sumner, Larry Lynch, Mel Watkins, Lynn Trainor, and Robin Harris. Art Kruger and I attended their first meeting as "reactionary" observers.

For some years the Caucus was to press the faculty association to support demands of student organizations for a wider consultative role in the University, especially on matters of faculty appointment and tenure. On other issues the Reform Caucus was divided. Some of its members were militant opponents of the administration on issues of collective bargaining. Others deplored what they saw as the naked self-interest of UTFA on salary and benefit issues. The Reform Caucus never attracted strong faculty support, and nothing substantial was to come of its interest in a student-faculty alliance. Perhaps its main achievement was to keep alive a voice of dissent inside the faculty association on a number of issues, as well as keep some members active in the Association who might otherwise have left. Eventually the remnants of the Reform Caucus were to play a considerable role in promoting some of the equity issues of the 1980s, such as pay equity for women, stringent procedures in cases of sexual harassment, and improved security for non-tenured faculty.

Another echo of earlier hopes is evident in the active interest the faculty association showed for a year or two in the election of faculty members to the new Governing Council. Especially during Jim Conacher's presidency of UTFA in 1971-72 the faculty association endorsed candidates in most constituencies. The effort to elect candidates sympathetic to the faculty association's views was generally successful, and there was, for a time, some regular consultation between the UTFA executive and faculty members of the Governing Council. As the Governing Council established its procedures, however, it became clear that most of its faculty members did not relish being seen as representatives of the faculty association, and as faculty disillusionment with the Governing Council grew, the UTFA attempt to influence membership on the Council was abandoned.

Jim Conacher continued for a time, though with growing pessimism, to try to influence the new Governing Council. In August, 1972 he and Mike Uzumeri, the incoming President of UTFA, met with Malim Harding, the Chairman of the Governing Council and a former member of the Board of Governors. Harding was, on the whole, less unsympathetic to faculty interests than his successors in the chair of the Governing Council, but he told Conacher and Uzumeri bluntly that University of Toronto professors were not popular, either at Queen's Park or with the public. They had, he said, "made a botch of their presentation to the Legislature" on the composition of the Governing Council, and they had "got the public's back up." So, after twenty years of sustained and frequently intelligent effort, the faculty association found itself without power or popularity at a moment when bleak times lay ahead for Canadian universities generally, and Toronto especially.

Chapter Five
A New Start

For many Toronto faculty members, especially in Arts departments, the University in the early 1970s was a dispirited and
dispiriting place. The chaotic expansion of the 1960s, the shat-
tering of the old curriculum, the incivilities of student radicals, the
collapse of the old governing structure, the patent hostility of politicians and much of the public towards the universities, Toronto in
particular—all of these pressed in upon faculty self-esteem.

The excitement of the late 1960s was gone. Limitless expansion
had been replaced by what seemed limitless contraction. From having
seemed briefly to be the centre of the provincial government's approv-
ing plans for a universally educated society, the universities, Toronto
in particular, had become a favourite whipping-boy for all that had
gone wrong with the hopes of the previous decade. Hardly a month
went by without some attack on the University, its faculty in particular, from the local press. Tenure was regularly denounced as a sinecure
for layabouts. The great concrete bulk of the Robarts Library, seen
only a couple of years before as a cathedral of the new society, was now
vilified by the right as a horrendous waste of taxpayers' money, and
by the left as a monstrous symbol of elitist arrogance and a blight on
the neighbourhood as well.

There were to be grimly practical consequences of the University's
new status as a kind of pariah. Earlier plans for further expansion,
especially of graduate teaching, were abruptly cancelled, and a freeze
was put on all new capital projects. The provincial government em-

barked on the relentless campaign of under-funding which was to tumble Ontario from near the top among Canadian provinces in per capita university expenditure to almost the bottom, where it still rests. With a decade of ravaging inflation, average faculty salaries at Toronto were to fall in the 1970s by twenty per cent in real terms. A radical shift in student interest away from Arts subjects and towards the professional schools left many departments in Arts and Science with declining enrollment and real fears of faculty redundancy beyond the power of tenure to protect.

Nor was the menacing hostility that many Toronto professors felt around them wholly external. The noisy wave of radical student protest against the irrelevance of traditional academic disciplines had largely passed, and student discontent now expressed itself only in sullenness, but in the new Governing Council student and lay members routinely denounced what they saw as the elitist pretensions of professors.

The first president of UTFA, Jim Conacher, who only a few years before had been among the most active and hopeful advocates of a faculty-run university, now reported to the faculty association in tones increasingly pessimistic and gloomy. It was his opinion that "relations with the central administration have deteriorated"; the administration showed little interest in faculty opinion; the disregard of faculty interests was having a "serious effect on faculty morale"; some faculty members "question whether they want to remain at the University of Toronto." A number of scholars of some reputation did, indeed, leave the University. Many, however, left more subtly without leaving formally. They continued to do their work and meet their classes, but simply opted out of the University community. By the early 1970s the old University, good and bad, hierarchical and collegial, tediously and devotedly engaged in its processes, was dead.

One casualty of this decline was Claude Bissell. He retired as President of the University in 1971, though he had expected to stay longer. For a year Jack Sword, not himself an academic, was Acting President as he had also been in 1967-68 when Bissell was at Harvard. In 1972 a new President was appointed. This was John Evans, a medical researcher who had made a name for himself administratively as an innovative Dean of Medicine at McMaster.

Evans was to do little to reassure his alienated faculty. Though himself a Toronto alumnus, Evans neither had nor pretended to have the kind of devotion to the University that Bissell had had. He was a brisk and ambitious man whose style was managerial rather than collegial, and who gave the impression of viewing his presidency of the University as a step in his career rather than as its culmination. He was never at ease with the faculty and never popular with the faculty as a whole. Coming to the University at the end of the days of student radicalism, he made the mistake of many university presidents in the early 1970s—he took the question of relations with student organizations and the response to student demands more seriously than he need have done, and took faculty interests less seriously than he should have done.

To be fair to Evans, he had strengths which many faculty members failed to appreciate. He was an impressive and sometimes effective advocate of the University in the wider community. Internally he reformed and tightened the central administration, clearing up much of the inefficient confusion of overlapping and often incompetent decision-making which Bissell's casual and ad hoc administration had left behind. For the first time, the administration began to show professional skill in managing the University's limited and shrinking resources.

The weakness of the Governing Council allowed, if it did not compel, Evans to concentrate power ever more in Simcoe Hall. Indeed it was in the Evans years that "Simcoe Hall" became a University term for the central administration—radically simplifying and replacing a whole group of terms that in former times had been used to define power in the University—Faculty Council, College Council, Senate, President, Board of Governors. If Evans's reforms possessed the inherent efficiency of centralization, their weakness lay in their narrowness of consultative scope. Evans established what he called the "Simcoe Circle"—a group of central administrators who generated, traded, and discussed proposals among themselves. The Circle has disappeared, but the dangerously constricted circularity of consultation implicit in it remains a characteristic of the University's administration to this day.

The faculty association during Conacher's presidency faced the general hostility towards professors, both inside and outside the University, firmly but defensively—reacting more often than acting. Conacher criticized the administration for its responsiveness to student demands and neglect of faculty interests, and was, in turn, denounced by student leaders and by the Faculty Reform Caucus as a spokesman for outdated faculty pretensions.

Conacher was succeeded as UTFA President by Mike Uzumeri, who carried on similar policies, if somewhat more passively. Uzumeri was casual in his handling of Association business, meeting less frequently with his Executive than his immediate predecessors had done, or than his successors were to do. In some respects his presidency represented a return to the earlier concept of the office, as it had been perceived by the old ATS chairmen from the Sciences and professional faculties. Uzumeri, a civil engineer, was, in his collegial attitude towards the administration, his mistrust of faculty militance, his wariness of collective bargaining, the last of the old breed of faculty leaders.

Inevitably, given the budgetary cutbacks of the day and its own repudiation in 1970 of its efforts at serious collective bargaining, the faculty association was not successful in Conacher's and Uzumeri's years, 1971-73, in maintaining faculty salaries. The across-the-board increase for each of these two years was 3%, but, as the rise in cost-

78

of-living totalled only about 7.5% over this time, the salary erosion was insignificant, especially by comparison to that of the late 1970s. If the settlements were not as bad as they might have been, however, the procedures in "negotiating" them were atrocious. The faculty learned of the salary settlement for 1972-73, the second lowest at any Ontario university, from the pages of the Toronto *Star*. This represented a procedural discourtesy of which even Colonel Phillips and the old Board of Governors had never been guilty. Nevertheless, and rather oddly, the faculty association did make a real and substantial advance in its salary negotiations in 1972. This was the introduction of the progress-through-the-ranks (PTR) principle in calculating salary settlements.

During both Conacher's and Uzumeri's presidencies, the UTFA Salary and Benefits Chairman was Michael Finlayson. Finlayson was a young Australian who had done his Ph.D. in History at Toronto. He was neither militant nor of the left in the mould of Wayne Sumner, but he was a good-humouredly combative and persistent advocate of faculty interests. He had adapted the PTR formula from a scheme at Waterloo University and he argued tirelessly for its adoption at Toronto.

This formula separated salary increases into two parts—an economic increase, and a component representing merit and career progress. A separation of the components of salary increases had, of course, been proposed earlier, but the essence of Finlayson's PTR formula lay in the definition of the non-economic component. This had hitherto been seen merely as a merit increase, wholly discretionary in the hands of deans and directors. Finlayson argued that, for a faculty group, it represented simply the group's progress through the ranks from initial appointments at a low salary to senior professors' appointments at a salary averaging more than two-and-a-half times beginning salary.

Within such a group, some individual professors would progress further and faster than others. This disparity reflected "merit" awards. But for the group as a whole the progress was constant and, most important, should not be seen as representing a salary increase at all, since it represented only career progress and was retrievable as members of the group retired at relatively high salaries and were replaced by new members at low salaries. Thus, Finlayson argued, the PTR component should be taken as a first charge on the budget, should not be regarded as part of a salary increase, should be mandatory for a group (i.e., a department or small faculty), but discretionary for individuals.

The logic of Finlayson's argument was irrefutable, and he pursued his case relentlessly. The Budget Committee grudgingly accepted the principle, and in December, 1972 the Governing Council accepted it for a three-year trial. Though for years the administration misunderstood and sometimes misapplied it, and toyed with its abolition, the PTR component was gradually institutionalized and became a permanent feature, at least until now, of salary settlements at Toronto.

The consequences of the PTR formula's adoption were very considerable, not all of them foreseen at the time. When combined with departmental (and small faculty) profile tables which allowed individual faculty members to compare their "merit" increases with those of (un-named) colleagues, the PTR scheme radically reduced the opportunities for wildly disparate and inequitable awards by chairs, deans, and directors. Inevitably "merit" awards became more formulaic and even mechanical. This was not, in all cases, beneficial. It has probably tended to reward steady, productive mediocrity in scholarly achievement more than should be the case, and to discourage major rewards for major achievements. But it has, at the same time, forced administrators to be far more accountable in salary matters than they had been.

Inflation over the past two decades has also affected the PTR in at least two unforeseen ways. As originally conceived, the PTR component of an individual's average increase in pay was expected to be roughly half the total and the economic increase half. But inflation has, in fact, meant that the economic increase has in most years been more, sometimes much more, than half the total increase for an individual. So the PTR component, and the merit increase included in it, has been of less weight than expected. Thus the principle that Bissell argued for in the 1960s, that most of a professor's salary increase should be discretionary, has been reversed, and most of it has been across-the-board.

Also, the argument Finlayson and others in the faculty association made that, over time, the PTR component would be a non-cost item in the University budget, as relatively well-paid senior professors retired and were replaced by people appointed at less than half their salaries, has not proved to be true. The relatively few appointments at the lower end of the salary scale have had to be made at a higher level than foreseen, and, as well, the great mass of faculty members appointed in the 1960s has not yet retired, and these members continue to receive PTR increases. So while the nominal cost of the PTR component has averaged a little over three per cent a year, only about a third has been retrieved by faculty rotation, and the actual cost to the university has been around two per cent a year, now down to about 1.5%. In years to come the University may well gain back much of this with the retirements of faculty members appointed in the 1960s. And, in any event, if inflation has adversely affected the University budget in respect to the PTR component, it has benefitted the University at faculty expense in other respects, notably in the cost of funding pensions.

A final effect of regarding the PTR component as no part of the salary increase is somewhat intangible, but of considerable psychological importance. It has made the average salary increase for a given year seem smaller than otherwise would be the case. Or, to put it the other way, when what came to be called the PTR component was included in the announced annual increase, the increase seemed larger than it was. In the 1960s, for example, the seven per cent annual increases were not really seven per cent at all, but three or four per cent, the rest being a concealed component representing career advancement. As the University administration, and the Toronto press, got used to discussing salary increases without the PTR component, their slightness became evident. Probably, over the past twenty years, salary settlements at Toronto would have been measurably lower if the PTR component had not been removed from them.

In considering the faculty association during the early 1970s, the adoption of the PTR formula is particularly striking since, in nearly every other respect, the faculty association's prospects seemed dismal. There is perhaps one rather curious qualification that should be made to this assertion. That arises from the very processes that had produced the new governing structure of the University and nullified the old hopes of a faculty-run university. These processes had destroyed or diminished the former agencies of faculty power and influence—the college and faculty councils, the network of informal faculty consultation with senior administrators, the University Senate. The faculty association was all that was left. So, in ways that were perhaps not always desirable, UTFA became the only major repository of faculty influence and very nearly the only voice of the faculty, not merely in salary and benefit questions, but in all matters of faculty concern—appointments policy, teaching loads, tenure, academic freedom, University affairs generally.

John Evans himself helped legitimize an augmented role for the faculty association by the narrowness and formality of his own consultation with faculty members. While Bissell had always, sometimes rather testily, regarded the faculty association as only one of a number of sources of faculty opinion, Evans regarded it as the only faculty body he had an obligation to inform or consult. To be sure, his consultation was usually perfunctory and, at least in the first years of his presidency, less serious than his consultation with student organizations. But at least he did inform and, in minor matters, consult UTFA, and gradually the faculty association and the faculty became largely indistinguishable to most people inside the university community.

I had been Uzumeri's vice-president and agreed to accept nomination for the UTFA presidency for 1973-74, and was duly acclaimed. Until 1981 when there was a contested election, the faculty association president was always acclaimed. There was in those days a complicated, somewhat oligarchical, procedure for choosing members of an incoming president's executive committee. Nominations were in the hands of the immediate past-president of the Association, in the case of my Executive, Jim Conacher, Uzumeri's predecessor. It seemed to me that the president should have something to say about his Executive, so I pressed Conacher to nominate an executive committee of my choosing. He agreed, a little reluctantly in the case of my choice for vice-president, Pat Rosenbaum from the English Department, known as a strong advocate of faculty collective bargaining. Rosenbaum's nomination produced a revolt of conservative members of the UTFA Council, led by Uzumeri. They produced a second nomination, that of Keith Yates from Chemistry, and Yates was elected over Rosenbaum by one vote. Rosenbaum was understandably indignant at the Council's action, as was I. As it turned out, however, Yates, who had known nothing of the contest in the Council, proved to be a loyal and effective member of my Executive. There was some Lancashire scepticism in his attitude towards formal collective bargaining, but he and I got on well and were in agreement on most issues. His presence on the Executive was usefully reassuring to some conservative colleagues.

Though I certainly had no plan of action for the Association when I became President, it did seem to me that we needed somehow to reassert a credible claim to faculty influence in the University. Reacting to student and lay attacks seemed pointless. What we needed clearly was to be able to engage Simcoe Hall in serious collective bargaining. This was difficult, however, because of our own earlier renunciation of such action, and also because the financial climate was unfavourable.

Indeed, the University administration was engaged in what seemed at the time an attack on tenure itself. Evans had set up a Presidential Task Force chaired by the Provost, Don Forster, to review the Haist Rules and the whole process of granting and maintaining tenure. There was serious talk of five-year reviews of all appointments, of a freeze on making new tenured appointments, of subjecting the whole professoriate to tighter administrative control on fiscal grounds.

In 1972-73 I had chaired an UTFA committee on the Presidential Task Force and engaged Forster in a considerable dialogue in meetings and in correspondence. We argued, of course, for the maintenance of tenure and of a normal appointments policy and, as well, following new CAUT guidelines, for greater faculty control over appointments and tenure decisions. In the event, the Task Force's recommendations were moderate, involving mainly a tightening up of procedures for granting tenure, along with the beginnings of what later became an effective procedure for appealing negative tenure decisions.

Early in 1974 we sent a questionnaire to the membership asking their views on appointments, tenure, promotion, and dismissal for fiscal reasons. About 700 members returned this questionnaire. On criteria for granting tenure and promotion, members thought demonstrated scholarly achievement and effectiveness in teaching were of essentially equal importance, and thought nothing else (e.g., univer-

sity service in administration and on committees, and community
service) was of any significance.

We asked what, if the University was faced with a grave financial
crisis, members found preferable: (1) closing marginal parts of the
University; (2) dismissal of redundant staff throughout the University; or (3) across-the-board salary reductions. Respondents divided
fairly equally among these three unpalatable choices, though more
(40%) favoured salary reductions than favoured the others. Asked
their views on the possible dismissal of staff for fiscal reasons, members divided quite equally between those (48%) who thought dismissals should take place on academic grounds alone from among tenured
and untenured staff, and those (52%) who thought dismissals should
take place first from among untenured staff. In what was perhaps less
surprising in 1974 than it would be now, 50% of respondents thought
the presence of a graduate student on a tenure committee either
desirable or acceptable; two-thirds of respondents, however, found
the presence of an undergraduate on such a committee unacceptable.

As it turned out, the gloomiest forebodings of the early 1970s did
not come to pass. There were no wholesale dismissals; tenure remained intact. The decline of University funding, however, went on
through the decade and beyond—a slow, tearing pressure on the
fabric of the University. And much of the contraction was paid for by
the faculty, which through the uncompensated effects of inflation, did
suffer an across-the-board cut in real salary of more than twenty per
cent.

The bleak times of the early 1970s had a good deal to do with the
emergence of another issue, though it sprang from other sources as
well. This was the question of Canadianization in the universities. In
a broad sense this concern was part of the nationalist reaction against
American domination of Canada, but it was given particular force by
the contraction of the universities and consequent unavailability of
new university appointments for Canadians. Beginning with the pub-

lication in 1971 of James Steele's and Robin Mathews's *Struggle for Canadian Universities*, this matter came more and more under discussion. CAUT took it up and eventually called for restrictions on the appointment of non-Canadians to new university positions. It was, for some time, a divisive and distracting issue.

In UTFA colleagues divided on this matter quite differently than on most other issues. Some of the people I worked closely and harmoniously with on all other questions were ardent nationalists and favoured national and thus non-academic criteria for new appointments. The majority of us argued for the retention of academic qualifications as the sole criterion for making appointments. We quarrelled with CAUT on this, and, indeed, Michael Finlayson and I walked out of the Annual Meeting of CAUT in 1975 in protest of their endorsement of hiring restrictions on national grounds. It still seems to me that on this issue CAUT was wrong and we were right, though frequently it had been the other way round.

In March of 1974, quite suddenly, something alarming happened at the University, of which, in the event, we were able to make good use. This was what, at the time, was called the Banfield Crisis. Edward Banfield was an American political scientist who, in his work in urban studies, had criticized government expenditure on welfare as ineffective in dealing with the problems of the urban poor. His views were controversial, and popular with the political right. He was invited to speak at Toronto by the American Studies Committee which sponsored an annual visit by a distinguished scholar in some aspect of American history or political science. His visit was a kind of red flag to the far left on the Toronto campus, especially to the Students for a Democratic Society, a somewhat ragtag and disreputable remnant of the group of that name which had, a few years earlier, been a formidable and serious radical force on American campuses. The local SDS had disrupted meetings of the Governing Council earlier in the year, and denounced Banfield as a racist, which he was not, and threatened to "run him off the campus" if he came to Toronto.

At UTFA we urged the University administration to defend Banfield's right to speak and to take proper disciplinary action against any who might attempt to disrupt his lectures. The administration refused to take our warnings seriously and offered a cloudy justification for doing nothing on the grounds that they did not want to polarize the University "community" by taking disciplinary action against any group. The University officer directly responsible for this policy was my erstwhile colleague in the History Department, Jill Conway, Vice-President for Internal Affairs, who was shortly to leave the University to become President of Smith College. Her only recommendation in regard to Banfield's visit was that he be invited to postpone it. With no University protection, Banfield was prevented from finishing his first lecture, threatened with physical attack at the end of his second, and prevented from speaking at all at his third appearance. At his second lecture he had to be given physical protection by faculty volunteers.

There was real faculty outrage at the administration's indifference to the fundamental right of free academic speech in the University. Immediately after Banfield's final attempt to speak, an angry group of faculty members, of whom I was one, confronted John Evans in his office and demanded action from him. The UTFA Council met the next day and passed unanimously a set of demands, notably that Evans issue "an explicit statement of the right of free discussion in orderly assembly of any academic question on this campus." We also demanded that Evans lay out in detail the steps the administration would take to ensure such free discussion, including the use of the University's disciplinary authority and, if necessary, the civil authority as well. We finally demanded that the President "respond satisfactorily" to our demands in one week's time.

Both in tone and in substance, UTFA's demands were unprecedented. They were, and were intended to be, harsh and uncompromising. The issue, simply and fundamentally the issue of free academic speech at the University, seemed to us to justify harsh action. The University administration's response was, on the one hand, to deprecate the tone and substance of the UTFA protest as uncollegial and overstated, but, at the same time, essentially to meet our demands, even as to the one-week time-limit for a satisfactory response.

Evans apologized to Banfield; disciplinary action was taken against students who had disrupted his lectures; and the administration quietly abandoned the shallow communitarian slogans by which it had justified its role as a mediator among the various "estates" that made up the University. At the beginning of his presidency, Evans had assured the faculty that he regarded them as "one of the most important estates of the University." This chilling encomium was not to be repeated, and the administration began to treat the faculty association with a somewhat wary respect as, at least, a potentially dangerous antagonist.

The solid advantage to us of the administration's mishandling of the Banfield affair was that it enabled UTFA to hammer Simcoe Hall on an issue where we had whole-hearted faculty support. We were able to drive a wedge between many conservative faculty members and the administration they had habitually trusted.

Among the many letters and calls of support I received from faculty members, there were, it is true, three protests at our actions: one, criticizing the uncivil tone of our "ultimatum" to the administration, was from Adrian Brook in Chemistry. Another was from Don Chant, Chairman of the Zoology Department, with a "copy to President Evans"; Chant resigned from the faculty association, writing that he no longer wished to be a member of that organization "under the presidency of Professor Nelson"; the issue of academic freedom was a

real one, Chant wrote, "but to build it into a general attack on President Evans ... is unwarranted and uncalled for."

The third letter of protest was from Frank Iacobucci, who judiciously combined approval for our actions with criticism of our language and methods. It was not many months before Evans appointed
Chant Provost of the University, and, in due course, Iacobucci also
served in that office before leaving the University for a judicial career
that led eventually to a seat on the Supreme Court of Canada.

A means of communication with the faculty that proved useful to
us in the Banfield affair was the UTFA *Newsletter*. Newsletters of
various forms had been used on occasion by the faculty association,
but from September, 1973 we began to send one out more or less
regularly at monthly or bi-monthly intervals, reporting to members
on salary and benefits, and other issues, as well as reporting quickly
on extraordinary events like the Banfield business. I adopted a format
that Wayne Sumner and I had both used a couple of times in the
spring of 1970. In 1979, when he was President, Michael Finlayson
was to change the format, but the *Newsletter* has continued to be the
Association's chief regular means of reaching its members.

As might have been expected in the rigorous financial climate of
the early 1970s, more and more grievances were coming to the faculty
association from members—grievances principally over salary, dismissals, and denial of tenure. Grievances had, of course, always been
part of Association activities. In earlier days they had been infrequent,
and were dealt with discreetly by informal consultation between senior faculty and administrative officers of the University. For some
years members of the Law Faculty had assisted the Association in
advising grievors, originally on an occasional, casual, and informal
basis, and, later, more regularly.

By the 1970s we were having to ask a member of the Law Faculty
each year to act as a grievance counsellor. These colleagues were, on
the whole, remarkably obliging and dutiful in taking on this difficult

work. Probably, over a decade, a quarter or more of all the members of the Law Faculty assisted UTFA in grievance cases. In 1971 a regular Grievance Committee was established, chaired for some years by a member of the Law Faculty who frequently served as well on the UTFA Executive. The president of the Association was often also consulted by grievors, and we all had to learn the useful three-way distinction between the legitimacy of the grievor and that of the grievance, and between both and the procedures used or abused.

Without uniform procedures for dismissal and denial of tenure, and with no regular appellate procedure, grievances could be both complex and bizarre. There was, for example, the case of a member at Trinity College, who, in 1974, was dismissed for fiscal reasons and then, *subsequently*, given tenure—not in reversal of her dismissal, but in a fuzzy effort to improve her credentials for seeking other employment. The most protracted and ultimately perhaps the most instructive grievance case during this time was that of Peter Seary who, along with several others in the University College English Department, was denied tenure in 1972.

As a member of Wayne Sumner's militant Salary Committee in 1970, Seary already had some adversarial experience in dealing with administrators, and he appealed the decision and sought the support of the faculty association. His appeal was heard by a committee appointed by Archie Hallett, Principal of University College, and the denial of tenure was confirmed. Seary argued, however, that neither the committee that originally denied him tenure, nor the appeal committee, had been provided full and proper documentation, and further, that the appeal committee had had no power to recommend tenure.

The UTFA Grievance Committee, chaired by Frank Iacobucci, supported Seary's initial appeal, but accepted assurances from University College and senior members of the English Department that Seary had had a fair appeal, and declined to support his appeal against the second denial of tenure decision. The UTFA Executive, in May, 1973, refused further help to Seary who then turned to CAUT. Their Academic Freedom and Tenure Committee was hesitant at first, but, after receiving a letter from Northrop Frye, who had sat on the appeal committee, stating that, if that committee had had the power to do so, he would have voted to recommend tenure for Seary, finally accepted Seary's argument that he had not been granted a proper appeal.

CAUT reproached the University administration and, implicitly, UTFA as well. In 1974 we reversed ourselves and, following CAUT guidelines, took up Seary's case again. We joined CAUT in asking for a Presidential Review Committee to consider his appeal on procedural grounds; Evans eventually agreed and finally, in the fall of 1975, a new tenure committee, established on the recommendation of the Review Committee, unanimously recommended reinstatment and tenure for Seary.

Seary's appeal, along with several others only slightly less contentious and protracted, made it clear, first, that we had been too casual and agreeable in dealing with the administration on grievances, second, that tenure and promotion committees required fuller documentation than they had been using, and finally, that we needed more regular and formal procedures for appeals against denial of tenure and dismissal. Fortunately, on this matter, there was a degree of common interest between UTFA and the adminstration. Simcoe Hall was sensitive to the threat of CAUT condemnation and, as well, wanted less abrasive and time-consuming means of disposing of grievances. In 1974, largely on the initiative of Don Forster, the Provost, the administration agreed to the establishment of a Tenure Appeals Committee. This Committee, following CAUT guidelines and precedents established by earlier grievance cases, worked well and was eventually institutionalized in the Memorandum of Agreement in 1977.

Given the cold institutional and political climate of the early 1970s, the faculty association probably did as well as it could have been expected to do in defending faculty interests. What we were not able immediately to do was establish effective collective bargaining. That was to require years of further effort.

Chapter Six

The Memorandum of Agreement

From 1973 to 1976, while I was President of the faculty association, our salary and benefits discussions with the administration made a little headway, creeping along, however, at a
glacial pace. In 1973 the UTFA Salary Committee was chaired by
Wendy Potter, a young, untenured member of the Psychology Department. The question of salary equity for women was finally beginning to be taken seriously in the University, and Wendy Potter worked
especially hard on this issue. The faculty association had been slow to
take it up.

In the fall of 1971 at a general meeting Michael Finlayson, then
chairing Salary and Benefits, had been asked about comparative salaries for men and women and had replied that "no study had been done
to compare them." In the spring of 1972 Finlayson was asked again
about this and had said that in the following year "a woman would be
on the Committee ... and would be concerned with this." Since two
women had served on the Salary Committee as early as 1954, this did
not in itself represent a radical step forward. But this time the issue
did not go away, and, within two years, the University had set up an
Anomalies Committee which, in 1976, for example, considered salary
inequities for thirty-three women and recommended adjustments for
most of them. Adequate provision for maternity leave also became a
serious issue in 1976.

Wendy Potter also worked to provide evidence of the steady deterioration of salaries generally and, within the constraints of our mis-

erably unsatisfactory negotiating procedures, was effective. We had two meetings with the Budget Committee in the late summer and fall of 1973 and presented our arguments for an across-the-board increase of 11.5%. Maintaining what Michael Finlayson had called the "Alice-in-Wonderland quality" of these meetings, members of the Budget Committee listened to us, asked a question or two and otherwise stayed silent. After the second meeting, President Evans invited Wendy Potter and me to meet with him and Don Forster and, at this meeting, offered to give us figures for the salary settlement the Budget Committee would recommend, but only on condition we inform no one else, not even other members of the Salary and Benefits Committee or the UTFA Executive. Of course, we refused this offer. The UTFA Council promptly agreed to our recommendation that we stop pretending we could discuss benefits with the administration and break off these discussions.

In a letter to Evans, I wrote, "You tell us the Budget Committee is not free to discuss salary with us. Tell us then with whom we can carry on such discussion." The following spring Evans proposed a joint committee of members from the administration and members from UTFA to discuss benefit proposals. We agreed to this and finally had a mechanism for discussion though certainly not for negotiation. The Joint Committee, by the way, has continued to serve to this day as a vehicle of variable utility for discussions between the administration and UTFA.

By 1974 the Consumer Price Index which had already been rising sharply for over a year was soaring; for a couple of years it increased at a rate averaging nearly one per cent a month. Our salary settlement for 1974-75 of 7% across-the-board thus meant a fall in real wages of about 4% for the year. Faced with a salary decline that threatened to become catastrophic, our new Salary and Benefits Chairman, Ken Bryden, drew up a well-argued proposal for a 25% across-the-board increase for 1975-76, roughly half to compensate for loss of real income in recent years and half to keep up with the anticipated rise in the CPI. Bryden was a political scientist and a long-time socialist and NDP activist. He was thoroughly used to challenging established power and losing. He combined a calm rationality in argument with a good-humoured scorn for opponents' arguments weak in logic but impregnably defended by established authority.

Although our demand for a 25% increase was not out-of-line with recent salary settlements for teachers and in the private sector, it was denounced by the Toronto press and by student organizations at the University as a further example of faculty arrogance and greed. In our joint-committee discussions we did eventually lower our proposal to 18%, the administration offering 9%.

By this time we were beginning to have something like negotiations at a bargaining table, though without any means of resolving an impasse. In the spring of 1974 John Evans had offered his own services as a final arbiter. The following year the administration reluctantly agreed to mediation, insisting, however, that the mediator be from inside the University and that he have no power to make his own recommendation. Our mutually agreeable "mediator" that year was Art Kruger who, predictably, was unable to bring us and the administration together. The administration finally imposed a settlement with a 12% increase.

The following year, 1976, with Bryden again our Salary Chairman, and with inflation abating slightly, we pressed Evans to agree to an outside mediator. He turned this proposal over to Frank Iacobucci, now Vice-Provost, and Iacobucci agreed to an outside mediator but not to our demand that he might make (non-binding) recommendations of his own. Rather, Iacobucci proposed, the mediator, failing agreement, would simply report the final position of each side to the other. We finally agreed to this and agreed to Owen Shime as mediator. Shime was an experienced professional mediator and arbitrator, and was successful in bringing us and the administration fairly close, but we failed in the end to come to terms, and accepted another imposed settlement, this time of 8.4% across-the-board with a few additional benefits which Shime's mediation had been helpful in getting.

During these years, despite our failure to achieve arbitration or even full mediation, we were inching ahead procedurally in our discussions with the administration. On both sides, our presentations were becoming more elaborate and precise. We were now, for example, routinely setting the cost of other benefits against the economic increase under discussion. To engage in these discussions we were straining our own resources. The UTFA office still had only one part-time employee. The Salary and Benefits Chair received neither released time nor any other compensation. In these years, probably more than either earlier or later, we were dependent on both CAUT and OCUFA for salary and cost-of-living data and other information. With Shime's mediation in the spring of 1976, it was apparent that our procedures had gone about as far as they could go informally. We were faced either with abandoning our attempt at effective collective bargaining or fixing it in some contractual form.

The question of formal collective bargaining, either under a voluntary agreement or in an agreement reached by a bargaining unit certified by the provincial Labour Relations Board, was not seriously considered at Toronto until the fall of 1974. By this time, of course, faculty "unionization" had become increasingly commonplace elsewhere in Canada, as well as in the United States and Britain. Certified unions were also becoming more the rule than the exception elsewhere in the public service.

By early 1975 faculty unions were certified bargaining agents at most of the Quebec universities, at a number of small English-speaking universities as well as at the University of Manitoba, and in a number of state university systems in the United States. By the following spring about a third of all Canadian faculty members, including about a third of Ontario faculty, were in certified bargaining units. At Toronto, however, these gusty winds of change barely stirred the air, at least initially. Especially in Science departments and in well-established professional faculties, and among senior faculty generally, there was still an almost visceral aversion to the use of "trade union tactics" by professors.

At UTFA two things were clear to us: first, that if we could not persuade a majority of our members that certification was, at least, worth considering, we would have little credibility in pressing the administration even for a voluntary agreement to bargain collectively. But, second, if we got too far ahead of the membership in advocating a collective agreement, we could easily be repudiated. We decided to move ahead, but with some caution. As a preliminary step, it seemed useful to try to determine how the process of faculty "unionization" was working elsewhere at universities that were in some ways comparable to Toronto. So, in September, 1974, Keith Yates, still the Vice-President, and I went out to Winnipeg and Vancouver to see what we could learn from faculty association activities at the Universities of Manitoba and British Columbia. I also went to Saskatoon, where the faculty at the University of Saskatchewan was in the process of certifying, but it was Manitoba and UBC that were most instructive.

At Manitoba we found an agreement reached by a certified faculty union in place and working reasonably well. The people there on the faculty association executive seemed efficient, well-organized, and appeared to command faculty confidence. The drive for certification had, however, been resisted in some of the professional faculties and some of these had eventually been left out of the certified bargaining unit. At UBC a rather narrow majority of the faculty had voted to certify, and we found a good deal of division of opinion and even bitterness. The association executive was hard-working and enthusiastic, but some of its members appeared to be professionally insecure and to lack the support of many of their colleagues. The prospects of a united faculty union did not seem bright and, not long afterwards, the UBC faculty voted to seek de-certification. Eventually the faculty association there settled with the administration on a voluntary agreement.

So far as certification was concerned, Manitoba's experience seemed mildly encouraging, and British Columbia's somewhat discouraging. There were clearly cautionary lessons to be learned from both. Shortly after returning from the West, we set up a Collective Bargaining Committee to consider some of the problems of a formal bargaining agreement with the University. I chaired this committee and Ken Bryden served on it, but we chose the other members deliberately to represent conservative departments in Arts and Science and some of the stronger professional faculties. These members were Bert Allen, the former Dean of Arts and Science, from Chemistry; Noah Meltz from Economics; David Beatty from the Law Faculty; Mike Uzumeri from Engineering; and, later, John Crispo from Management Studies. We met through the winter of 1974-75 and were able to agree finally on a report making two general recommendations: one was to seek legal advice on what was necessary to put the faculty association in a position to seek certification under the labour laws. The other was to ask the UTFA Council and membership to endorse a formula for merit and market salary differentials.

The problem of merit differentials was not too difficult; its solution was simply to agree that salary settlements did not impose ceilings, and that individual members could negotiate beyond a settlement for better salaries and benefits. The differential salaries paid in some of the professional faculties whose members were in high demand outside the University posed a more difficult problem. Here we recommended that existing market differentials be endorsed in any collective bargaining contract, along with fairly permissive guidelines in regard to outside income, and that subsequent changes require amendment of the UTFA constitution, that is, a two-thirds majority at a general meeting. The UTFA Council and, later, a general meeting endorsed these recommendations, and this, along with the Collective Bargaining Committee's credibility in the departments and faculties most affected, may have gone some way to head off the kind of opposition to a collective bargaining agreement that had developed at other universities in Science and professional faculties.

Following the Collective Bargaining Committee's recommendations, we sought legal advice on what was necessary to put UTFA in a position to seek certification as a faculty bargaining agent, should we wish to do this. We engaged the services of Jeffrey Sack, a young labour lawyer who, with his colleagues at Sack, Charney, Goldblatt, and Mitchell (now Sack, Goldblatt, and Mitchell), has advised the faculty association on various matters ever since. Sack thought the original purpose of the association, and the purposes defined in the constitution, qualified us as a potential bargaining agent for the faculty, but he thought we needed to clear ourselves of some degree of administrative taint. He advised us to deny membership to academic administrators above the level of chairs, and to define our constituency much more precisely than we had done. In particular, he did not like the "opt-out" means of defining our membership.

We accepted Sack's advice and terminated the "opt-out" scheme which we had negotiated with the administration a decade earlier and which had appeared to be useful in holding our membership. This required us, in the fall of 1975, to embark on an intense membership drive in order to recapture as signed-up members those who had hitherto been members automatically with their appointments. We were a little apprehensive about this, but, in the event, signed up as card-carrying members of UTFA almost exactly the same number, about 1550, as we had had under the opt-out formula. Though the totals were the same, there was a measurable shift within them: we gained about 200 new members, overwhelmingly from Arts departments, and lost about 200 old members, mainly from Engineering departments, Management Studies, and some Science departments, Chemistry and, especially, Botany and Zoology.

Another issue which had arisen in 1974 had, in the meantime, allowed us to expand our membership in another direction. This was the matter of membership for professional librarians. Partly in connection with the certification of faculty unions elsewhere in Canada and in the United States, many faculty associations had already admitted professional librarians to membership, and the Toronto Librarians' Association (LAUT) asked us, in the fall of 1974, to consider admitting them to UTFA. The national librarians' association had already asked CAUT to bargain for them where local faculty associations would not, and CAUT was reported to be sympathetic to this request.

There seemed to be sound reasons, both academic and practical, for admitting the librarians. They formed a compact group of scholarly colleagues with training, interests, and commitments closer to those of faculty than any other University group. We were already, in effect, bargaining for them, since our recent settlements were invariably models for theirs. As members, they would strengthen UTFA's negotiating position, especially if we were to move to certification. The chief argument against their admission was simply that they were not faculty members, and that their admission would cause confusion in respect to such questions as tenure, sabbatical leaves, and salary structure.

On balance, the arguments in favour of inviting the librarians to join us seemed to justify doing so, and the Executive recommended this action to the Council, which endorsed it. A general meeting in the spring of 1975 approved librarians' membership, and made the constitutional changes necessary to permit it. In the years that have followed, the librarians have probably made some gains as members of UTFA that would have been more difficult on their own. The salary ceilings for two ranks of librarians have been abolished, the

PTR formula has been fully applied to librarians' salary settlements, and they have developed a policy of scholarly leaves analogous to sabbatical leave for faculty. UTFA, as a whole, has gained a substantial and loyal body of additional members representing about seven per cent of total membership.

There was not much overt faculty opposition to the admission of librarians at the time, but, over the years, conservative colleagues have occasionally reproached me for "bringing them in" to UTFA. A few librarians think their particular identity and some of their issues have been obscured or lost in the larger unit. But, on the whole, it appears to have been a mutually agreeable union.

In 1975 and 1976 we did several other things as part of the process of putting our house in order in anticipation of possible certification. UTFA's income was wholly inadequate, virtually all of it going to CAUT and OCUFA. Our dues had risen, but were still assessed as a flat yearly amount, now based on rank. We were able to persuade the Council and the 1975 Spring Meeting to approve a new formula for collecting dues based, as OCUFA's and CAUT's were, on a mill rate. We set this at 0.4% of salary, and it represented a doubling of dues for the average member, rather more than that for the higher paid members of staff. The mill rate assured that income would rise automatically with salary increases, but, even so, it has had to be raised from time to time to its present level of 0.65%.

With an augmented income, even though it was soon to be eroded by raises in the CAUT and OCUFA mill rates, we were able to consider appointing a full-time person in the UTFA office with executive duties and a special responsibility for collective bargaining. There was no disagreement as to our need for a paid employee who could take some of the burden of work off the Salary and Benefits, and Grievance chairs, as well as the President; but we were not quite sure what sort of person we needed. There was some support for appointing an executive director, presumably an academic, with duties analogous to the executive directors of CAUT and OCUFA. Finally, however, we agreed to try to keep effective management of the Association in the hands of its elected officers, and to search for an executive assistant to the President. The first person appointed to this post was Diana Moeser, in June, 1976.

With a decline in the frequency of general meetings and a marked decline in attendance at them, the Council of the Association had become, or seemed as if it should become, more important. But the Council was a somewhat unsatisfactory body. It was seriously unrepresentative of the membership of the Association. Three-fifths of its members represented the professional faculties with, now, only about two-fifths of UTFA members. Thus, on average, each Council member from Arts and Science and the Colleges represented more than twice as many faculty members as each Council member from the professional faculties. In addition, the Arts and Science members were elected at-large, and had no responsibility for individual constituencies.

We asked Martin Mueller, who chaired the University Government Committee, to consider organizational changes. Mueller's committee came back with some fairly radical proposals. With a view to creating a large deliberative body that could, in some sense, replace the old general meeting, and using CAUT organization as a model, Mueller proposed replacing the Council with an "Assembly" of about eighty members elected from constituencies proportionate to their membership in UTFA. He also proposed replacing the Executive with a larger and more formal "Board."

Mueller's proposals were immediately and cogently attacked by a member of his committee, Stanley Schiff, the Council member from the Law Faculty. Schiff, incidentally, filled a useful and special role in his seventeen years on the UTFA Council. Although he served on the Executive briefly, he preferred being a back-bencher and often a one-man loyal opposition. Unlike far too many Council members, Schiff did his homework. He was always well-prepared and informed and, though sometimes wrong, and frequently a thorn in the side of the president of the day, he often strengthened and clarified our debates and resolutions, and restrained irresponsible executive action.

Schiff's criticism of Mueller's proposals was compelling. He argued that a body as large as the proposed "Assembly" would be very cumbersome, incapable of real debate, its nominal members not likely to be interested in or knowledgeable about Association affairs. He argued that the existing Council would have been more effective if it had been better used and more genuinely consulted by the President. (I had, it is true, frequently by-passed the Council as we got into preparations for serious collective bargaining, fearing the conservatism of some of the members from the professional faculties.) He went on to make the classic arguments in favour of virtual representation and to doubt whether we needed precise constituencies in Arts and Science. His own proposal was simply a modest increase in the number of Arts and Science Council members to be elected at-large.

In the end, we compromised; we abandoned the proposed "Assembly" and "Board," but did recommend a near-doubling of the Council from thirty to about fifty-five members, most of the increase assigned to Arts and Science, whose members were now to represent defined constituencies, usually departments. These proposals were approved at a general meeting in the spring of 1976. In the years that have followed, though there does not appear to have been a radical change in the character of the Council, it has become more militant than the old Council in confronting the University administration, and it has been possible, at moments of crisis, for its members to inform and consult their constituents much more effectively than in the past.

In a variety of ways, we tried in 1975 and 1976 to bring the issues of collective bargaining to the attention of the membership. The *Newsletter* was especially useful for this, of course, but we also used press interviews, held study sessions, and discussed problems of certification at general meetings. In the fall of 1975 John Crispo and I debated the merits of seeking certification at a well-attended special meeting.

By the spring of 1976, the issues seemed familiar enough to UTFA members to justify a questionnaire on the subject. Nearly 900 members answered the questions we asked. By nearly two-to-one they supported "a more formal process of collective bargaining" with the University administration; by two-to-one they opposed seeking immediate certification; by nearly two-to-one they favoured seeking a voluntary collective bargaining agreement; by a narrow majority they favoured certification if a voluntary agreement was denied by the administration. Though members from some of the professional faculties and from some of the Science departments were less militant than their colleagues elsewhere in the University, the results of the questionnaire were generally consistent, and the message was a clear mandate for UTFA to seek a voluntary agreement.

With our various housekeeping changes accomplished, and with instructions from the membership to seek a voluntary bargaining agreement, it was a good time for a change in the UTFA Executive, most of whose members had served with me for two, some for three, years. It seemed to us that in order to assure as much faculty unity as possible in the negotiations that lay ahead, UTFA should have a new Executive dominated by people who had standing in the University and who had not been recently active in faculty association affairs. I was fortunately able to induce three such people to come on to the Executive for 1976-77. One was the Chairman of the Physics Department, Jim Daniels. Daniels had, a few years before, chaired a group that called itself the Committee of Concerned Faculty, and had attempted to mediate between the faculty association and student organizations. He had not been active in UTFA and had the confidence of some of the more conservative faculty members in Science departments. At the same time, he had become convinced that we should proceed towards certification unless a strong voluntary agreement could be reached. He accepted nomination for the UTFA presidency and was duly acclaimed.

The other two "newcomers" were Jean Smith and Harvey Dyck, neither of whom had been especially active in the faculty association. Smith was a political scientist, a native Mississippian, soft-spoken and confidential in manner, but hard-edged underneath. He had just finished playing a central role on a University committee, nominally chaired by Don Chant, that had negotiated the first collective agreement with the GAA, the teaching assistants' union, and he thought it a good time to try for a faculty contract. He thought a voluntary agreement could be reached, but was willing to go to certification if necessary. He agreed to chair the Salary and Benefits Committee. Harvey Dyck was a Mennonite of Manitoba origins, a colleague of mine in the History Department. I had been impressed with his political judgment and his grasp of University issues, and he, too, had decided it was a propitious time to press for a bargaining agreement. He agreed to come on to the Executive as Secretary.

Smith wasted no time setting up his "Salary and Benefits" Committee, really a collective bargaining committee of twenty members. He chose its members carefully, with a view to representing a wide spectrum of faculty interests and opinions, wisely excluding only those of us who had been most recently active in UTFA affairs. He was able, for example, to persuade Adrian Brook, Chairman of the Chemistry Department and a perennial critic of the faculty association, to serve; Brook had served with him on the GAA negotiating committee and he and Smith had a good relationship. As UTFA stalwarts and former presidents, Jim Conacher, Fred Winter, and Mike Uzumeri were invited to be members. In addition to Uzumeri, Hal Smith and Ken Smith represented Engineering. Peter Fitting, a leader in the Faculty Reform Caucus, and David Gauthier represented more radical Arts members. Finally, Smith persuaded a strong contingent of women to serve on his committee: Lorna Marsden, the new UTFA Vice-President; Carole Weiss (later Carole Moore) from the Library; Chaviva Hosek from English; and Mary Eberts from the Law Faculty. With the united support of such a committee, Smith felt he had little to fear from faculty opposition.

Using the GAA contract as a rough guide, Smith drafted a collective bargaining agreement himself. He worked his committee hard through the summer of 1976—it met more than twenty times into the early fall. Smith would bring a draft section of the agreement to the committee, which would discuss and sometimes amend or change it, but usually accept it in substance. At the next meeting, Smith would have another section for consideration. And so on, until the draft contract was finished in September. Smith then circulated the Draft Agreement to the whole body of faculty members and librarians, asking for their approval. There were 1354 ballots counted, 944 in favour of the Agreement, 407 opposed; the percentage of approval ranged from 73% in Arts and Science to 63% in the professional faculties, and was 70% overall. To reassure any doubters as to the accuracy of his referendum, Smith persuaded The Hon. Mr. Justice Horace Krever of the Ontario Supreme Court to count the ballots along with Archie Hallett, Principal of University College, and Peter Russell from Political Science.

The Draft Agreement was fairly comprehensive. It laid out formal and binding grievance procedures, as well as detailed procedures for salary and benefit negotiations with binding third-party arbitration to resolve differences. It defined working conditions, workloads, leave policy, and a range of "civil rights" for faculty members and librarians, including academic freedom, freedom from discrimination, and the right of access to personnel files. It incorporated the Haist Rules guaranteeing faculty tenure. It clearly defined the academic status of librarians and extended tenure to them. It provided for child-care and adoption leave, and for a major improvement in maternity leave benefits. These, along with its other provisions, made the Draft Agreement as strong as, or stronger than, most of the agreements reached by certified unions on which it was modelled.

Armed with the results of his referendum, Smith then tackled the administration and the Governing Council. In early November Jim Daniels reported the referendum results to Mrs. Marnie Paikin, Chair of the Governing Council, and formally requested, on behalf of UTFA, that the Governing Council strike a negotiating committee. On November 18, the Governing Council authorized a committee to negotiate with UTFA; it was chaired by Don Chant, the Provost; its other members were Frank Iacobucci, Art Kruger, Milton Israel, and Ralph Barford, a lay member of the Council. It was another month, however, before the Governing Council furnished this committee with guidelines for its discussions. Smith chaired his negotiating team, the other members of which were Ken Smith, Charles Hanly, Carole Weiss, and Mary Eberts.

Negotiations began on the 21st of December and were continued through twenty-one meetings until March 8, 1977. Smith was deliberately harsh and uncompromising at the beginning, in order to preclude any attempts by the other side at collegial co-option. The administrative members found this tactic somewhat offensive, but understood the message. As meetings progressed, the atmosphere became relaxed and even, sometimes, congenial.

The committee went through the Draft Agreement clause-by-clause, Chant's side making no specific proposals, but raising various objections, seeking clarification, discussing alternatives. It seemed to Smith that they were gradually making headway. But on March 7, the administration suddenly produced an alternative draft, in which most matters of real substance, especially grievance procedures, were put aside to be considered later by Presidential advisory committees. On the crucial matter of salary and benefit negotiations, the administration's draft agreement provided for non-binding mediation, and left the final decision wholly to the Governing Council. On the day after presenting this document, Chant announced that his side could not discuss grievances, working conditions, workloads, leave policy, or salary and benefit negotiations. The Governing Council, Chant said, could not negotiate away its responsibility and powers to govern the University.

Smith was truly surprised. What, he wondered, had both sides been talking about through twenty-one meetings? He could only surmise that the other side had merely been trying to feel out faculty opinion with no commitment to real negotiation, or, perhaps, that Evans had finally drawn his side up sharply. Members of Chant's team recall nothing anomalous or inconsistent in their actions, and see their draft agreement as simply representing what their guidelines from the Governing Council allowed them to agree to. The truth of the matter probably was that, as had happened so frequently in salary discussions, the UTFA representatives thought they were negotiating, while the other side saw their meetings as mere discussion, and assumed that the ultimate decision was theirs.

With the unanimous support of the UTFA Council, Smith broke off negotiations and appealed for faculty support in another referendum in which respondents were asked simply whether or not they had confidence in the UTFA negotiators. More than 1500 ballots were returned, 150 more than in the poll the previous fall. Support for the UTFA position was about 88%, markedly higher than in the fall, and certainly enough to silence a few administrators and members of the Governing Council who were claiming that the UTFA negotiators did not represent faculty opinion.

With this renewed evidence of faculty support, Smith was anxious to force the other side back to the table, but was uneasy about making the first move himself. It was now early April; the deadlock had lasted a month. So Smith approached Ralph Barford and suggested he might like to arrange for Smith and Chant to meet. Barford was a genial and straightforward businessman who, as the only lay member of Chant's team, had occasionally evidenced a little amusement or bemusement at the passions of the academic world. He agreed to Smith's suggestion. Smith and Chant reopened discussions informally and, over a couple of weekends, sketched out a new draft agreement.

Though modified in minor ways in its final form, the agreement Chant and Smith worked out together was essentially the Memorandum of Agreement, the voluntary collective bargaining agreement that, as altered in later years, still forms the contractual basis of relations between the University administration and Toronto faculty and librarians. In form and in the sequence of matters addressed, it follows the alternative draft which Chant had produced in March much more closely than it does Smith's original draft. In substance it reflects a series of compromises.

Chant gave in on a number of issues: a precise grievance procedure is laid out, much as in Smith's draft, though with final appeal to the Grievance Review Panel rather than to a board of arbitrators. A list of faculty rights is defined, including academic freedom, freedom from discrimination, the right of access to personnel files, equitable workloads and working conditions. Salary during research leaves was raised from 50% to 75% of regular salary, and requests for research leave after six years without leave "shall not be unreasonably denied." The UTFA demand for seventeen weeks' paid maternity leave was agreed to. Finally, although this was an administration proposal aimed at avoiding the incorporation in the Agreement of a number of contentious issues, it was agreed that a number of existing policies should remain intact unless they were changed by mutual agreement. These included the Haist Rules on academic appointments, tenure, and promotion, part-time appointment policy, procedures in appointing academic administrators, existing policy on supplemental income, policies regarding retirement age and short-term, long-term, and compassionate leaves. These came to be known as the "frozen policies" and the faculty association was to benefit measurably from its veto on changes in them.

But Smith made a number of concessions to the other side. Some were minor, but, in the case of the librarians, the detailed description of procedures and policies in Smith's draft was abandoned, and these questions were left for a Presidential Task Force to consider. The administration agreed to a clear definition of the academic status of librarians but not to their permanent appointment on the same terms as tenured faculty members. Policies concerning promotions and contractually limited term appointments were left for later consideration by a Presidential Task Force.

Most important, Smith had to give in on binding arbitration in salary and benefit settlements. The procedures in the new Agreement were similar to those in Smith's draft (except for the abandonment of "final offer selection" in arbitration), and an arbitrator's award was to be binding on the faculty association. But such an award would bind the University only if it was not rejected by the Governing Council. Smith accepted a potential veto of an arbitral award by the Governing Council, first, because the administration simply would not yield on this point, and, second, because he thought it gave the faculty the substance of binding arbitration, since the consequences of the Governing Council's rejection of an arbitrator's award would almost certainly be the immediate certification of a faculty union.

Taken all in all, the Memorandum of Agreement represented a major step forward for the faculty association in its relations with the University administration. The formal definition of fair and binding grievance procedures, formal mediation in salary and benefit negotiations, the delineation of faculty civil rights, the "frozen policies" which the administration could not change unilaterally—all of these put the faculty association in a far stronger position than it had ever held before.

Why did the University negotiators agree to the Memorandum? Part of the answer lay in the skill with which Jean Smith had carried on the negotiations, and especially his success in keeping undivided faculty opinion behind him. This required, above all, keeping conservative faculty opinion from straying towards the position of the University administration. In this, Smith was at his best—reasonable, reassuring, accessible, responsive, subtly flattering, and not above delivering an occasional cool reminder that the advocates of outright certification would certainly take over were he to fail.

Jim Daniels gave Smith his full support, even though he was a little sceptical about the utility of a voluntary agreement. His support was crucial in keeping the UTFA Executive and Council solidly behind Smith, and it required him generously to take a back seat to Smith during most of the year he was President. Ralph Barford's common sense was useful, not only in getting negotiations resumed after they had been broken off, but also in breaking the deadlock that developed at the very end of negotiations over the question of paid maternity leave. Chant himself managed to keep his rationality and good humour as he was severely pressed between Smith on the one hand, and John Evans on the other. Evans was an unwilling ally, for, while he disliked the Agreement and resisted it nearly to the end, he never used with any skill or suppleness the powers of his office to divide the faculty. Had the administration, for example, produced something like its draft agreement of March 7th six months earlier, and mobilized conservative faculty opinion behind it, the outcome might have been very different.

There was a final potent force at work in bringing the Memorandum of Agreement into being, one that those of us who had not thought a voluntary agreement possible had overlooked. That was a deep and persistent desire among senior academic administrators to retain their own credentials as faculty members, not to be crudely defined as "management." This could be seen among the members of

Chant's committee, among others in Simcoe Hall and in senior administration elsewhere in the University.

Within the administration, perhaps only John Evans himself, lacking as he was any strong collegial sentiments, was relatively indifferent to the prospect of faculty certification. The determination of senior administrators to avoid the clear, harsh division between management and labour implicit in faculty certification was, of course, only an aspect of the same sentiment among faculty members-at-large who shrank from certification. But this sentiment, on the management side, was, for once, useful to the faculty association.

Chapter Seven
Binding Arbitration

Toronto faculty seem initially to have regarded the Memorandum of Agreement with some satisfaction. The UTFA Council endorsed the Agreement without an opposing vote, though Lee Patterson, a member of the Executive and a militant advocate of certification, abstained. When the Agreement was submitted to the whole faculty in a referendum, 95% of respondents approved it. Membership in the Association increased sharply, by about 16%, in the first year after the Memorandum was signed. Most of the increase came from Arts and Science and the Colleges, but about a hundred new members joined from the professional faculties, many of them from Engineering departments where support for UTFA had been weak. Though active membership declined a little in 1979, and has fluctuated within a narrow range in subsequent years, it has remained remarkably stable for the past fifteen years at just under 70% of total eligible members.

Jean Smith succeeded Jim Daniels as President of UTFA in July, 1977 and was to serve for two years. During his first year, he resolved a nagging issue of relations with CAUT which had arisen in 1976, only to be faced with a sudden crisis in relations with the provincial faculty association, OCUFA. The underlying problem in Toronto's relations with both these organizations lay in the self-sufficiency and insularity of the Toronto Association, exacerbated in the mid-1970s by the growing and costly commitment of both CAUT and OCUFA to certification by various locals elsewhere.

Toronto had, and indeed still does have, a problem shared only with a few larger Ontario faculty associations such as that at the University of Western Ontario, of having to support an expensive local association as well as contribute both to an expensive provincial association and to CAUT. Associations at smaller Ontario universities had negligible local dues, and associations elsewhere in the country did not have costly provincial associations to support, except in Quebec where a special arrangement with CAUT permitted the provincial association, FAPUQ, to claim most of the dues which elsewhere went to CAUT. Only Toronto and a few other Ontario faculty associations, having rejected certification, were being asked to pay higher and higher dues to support OCUFA's and CAUT's services to certified and certifying associations.

In the spring of 1976 the OCUFA Executive had proposed a 50% increase in the OCUFA mill rate, from 1.0 to 1.5 mills. Since our mill rate had recently been set at 4.0 mills and the CAUT assessment was 1.6 mills plus a special levy that made it effectively about 1.8 mills, we had only about 1.2 mills, or about 30% of our income for our own expenses—this without the proposed increase in OCUFA dues.

We fought the proposed increase at the OCUFA Council meeting in May, 1976 and succeeded in getting it reduced to 0.2 mills, making the new OCUFA assessment 1.2 mills. The Executive then persuaded the UTFA Council to withhold 0.2 mills from our CAUT dues, so that our combined payments to both organizations would remain unchanged. We did this in an effort to induce CAUT to engage in more substantial cost-sharing arrangements with OCUFA than it was doing. We were on uncertain ground in arbitrarily withholding a portion of our dues from CAUT; among other things we were violating a provision of our own constitution. As a means of bringing pressure to bear on CAUT, however, the action seemed justified.

Over the following year UTFA and CAUT engaged in considerable discussion on this issue. The UTFA Executive asked Brough

Macpherson to chair a committee to study the benefits to UTFA of both CAUT and OCUFA. The Macpherson Report, in the spring of 1977, concluded that, in regard to CAUT's three main areas of operation, UTFA benefitted as much as any other local association from CAUT lobbying activities in Ottawa; Toronto also received significant services from their Committee on Academic Freedom and Tenure, though these services were less significant than for most Canadian universities, but Toronto benefitted much less than most local associations from CAUT services in collective bargaining.

In respect to OCUFA, Macpherson thought their salary and benefits and taxation information was useful to UTFA, as were their efforts to increase provincial funding for the universities. But their other activities, in the area of public relations, and in support of collective bargaining, were not useful to Toronto. The Macpherson Report reminded Toronto faculty of a moral obligation to support faculty organizations less strong than their own but seemed to imply that, on balance, CAUT was of more value to Toronto than OCUFA; the Report recommended that UTFA resume full payments to CAUT.

In the fall of 1977 CAUT agreed not to make any further special levies, and to give Toronto the benefit of the lowest of its slightly differential assessment rates, and UTFA agreed to pay withheld dues, and resume regular payments. But almost at the moment these difficulties with CAUT seemed to be resolved, a new problem arose with OCUFA. In the decade of its existence, OCUFA had never aroused the strong feelings, either of support or of occasional mistrust, that had characterized relations with CAUT. Most Toronto faculty members were simply indifferent to OCUFA; the UTFA Executive and Council had regarded OCUFA with an originally somewhat patronizing goodwill; Charles Hanly, a Toronto Philosophy professor, had been its first Chairman, and its headquarters were in an old house on the edge of the Toronto campus. But by the middle-1970s the resolute domination of OCUFA by representatives from the smaller Ontario

115

universities combined with the growing burden of OCUFA dues and the related commitment of OCUFA to the certification of faculty unions at smaller universities had begun to arouse resentment among some Toronto members.

Briefly in the fall of 1977, however, relations with OCUFA seemed about to improve. Harvey Dyck, who was still on the UTFA Executive as Secretary, had become Vice-Chairman of OCUFA and seemed in line to become Chairman in 1978. Dyck had thought for a long time that Ontario universities, including their faculty associations, could bring more effective political pressure to bear on the funding policies of the provincial government than they had done, and he saw OCUFA as a potentially useful tool in this effort.

Affairs at OCUFA were in some turmoil in the fall of 1977. Graham Murray, the executive assistant for some years, had come into conflict with the new Executive and had been obliged to take permanent leave. The executive secretary, Lillian Smith, had resigned. For a few months the business of OCUFA was handled mainly by the Chairman, Paul Cassano from Windsor, and Dyck, the Vice-Chairman. Dyck, strongly supported by Jean Smith, thought OCUFA could continue effectively to be run without a paid executive assistant, perhaps by buying released time for some members of the Executive. But among members of the OCUFA Executive from the smaller universities there was a strong sentiment for replacing Murray with a new paid official. Finally in March, 1978 the OCUFA Executive invited Dyck to run for the chairmanship of OCUFA, but, at the same time, agreed to appoint an executive vice-chairman at a salary of $46,000 a year.

As it happened, the salary proposed for the new executive vice-chairman almost exactly equalled UTFA's contribution to OCUFA. It also was more than all but a very few Toronto professors were paid—the average Toronto salary then was about $30,000. Dyck and Jean Smith were outraged, not only at what seemed to them the grandiosity of the proposed appointment, but at the casual over-riding by the Executive of the opposition of OCUFA's two largest supporters, Toronto and Western Ontario. Dyck refused to consider the OCUFA chairmanship and recommended to the UTFA Executive that Toronto cease paying dues and assume an "inactive status" in OCUFA. The Executive agreed, as did the UTFA Council after a last and rather unfriendly meeting with delegates from OCUFA. For a few months UTFA continued to pay a token $1000 per month to OCUFA and to use some OCUFA services. In the spring of 1979 even these payments were discontinued, and the breach was complete.

There was no outcry among Toronto members at the break with OCUFA and, in following years, it seemed to many that the divorce was final. The division in outlook and interests between UTFA and the representatives from smaller universities who continued to dominate OCUFA remained sharp.

But one disadvantage of Toronto's withdrawal from OCUFA did become apparent: to have two voices speaking at Queen's Park on behalf of Ontario faculty, one from Toronto and another from all the rest, seriously weakened whatever impact faculty associations might have on Provincial policy. Essentially for this reason UTFA, after five years on its own, re-opened negotiations with OCUFA. In February, 1983 the UTFA Council voted unanimously to apply to rejoin OCUFA subject to minor concessions that would benefit Toronto on weighted voting and a lowered mill rate. OCUFA agreed to these concessions, and Toronto resumed its membership. It was Harvey Dyck, now the UTFA President, who brought about the reconciliation. Dyck had, in fact, decided that he had been wrong in 1978 to press for withdrawal from OCUFA.

Jean Smith and his Executive and negotiating team approached salary and benefit negotiations in 1977-78 with a degree of expectancy. For the first time, in the Memorandum of Agreement, UTFA and the University administration followed defined procedures in their discussions. When the two sides proved unable to agree on major points, they proceeded to mediation. The mediator/arbitrator selected from an agreed list was Professor D.A. Soberman, former Dean of Law at Queen's University. Failing in his mediative efforts, Soberman made his recommendations for 1978-79 in a Report released in February, 1978.

On a number of issues Soberman supported UTFA demands: he recommended substantial increases in salary for two lower ranks of librarians; he recommended that the full PTR scheme be applied to tutors on the same basis as for tenured faculty, instead of a much more limited formula for merit increase then in place; he recommended University funding for a dental plan requested by UTFA; and he recommended University tuition exemption for dependents of faculty members and librarians, along with some other minor benefits. Soberman conceded that the UTFA demand for an 8.0% across-the-board salary increase was "reasonable," but he accepted and recommended the University's offer of 3.75% on grounds of his perception of the constraints of the University's budget.

At another time the Soberman award might have well seemed outrageously bad to the faculty association. In recommending acceptance of the University salary offer of 3.75%, Soberman assured that Toronto faculty would receive what is probably the worst salary settlement relative to the rate of inflation over the past forty years. It provided for a salary cut of nearly six per cent in real terms for the year, representing about a quarter of the fall in real income during a disastrous decade. At most other Canadian universities salary settlements for 1978-79 were at five or six per cent. Yet, then and to this day, Smith and others in his negotiating team defend the first Soberman award. Why? There appear to be several reasons. First, Smith and most faculty members for that matter wanted to believe that the Memorandum of Agreement was a success, and that its provisions for salary and benefit negotiations were workable. Second, despite the lowness of Soberman's salary recommendation, his Report was seriously criticized in the Governing Council and, for a time, it seemed possible the Governing Council would reject it because of its support for UTFA demands on issues other than salary. Finally, the spring of 1978 saw, in some respects, the nadir in the popularity of Ontario universities in the 1970s, and many Toronto faculty were in an apprehensive and uneasy mood about their future prospects.

In April, 1978 an editorial in the Toronto *Globe & Mail* attacked tenure for university faculty as "ineffective and inefficient." "It is an anachronistic measure," said the *Globe*, "which risks inhibiting the universities from reorganizing to meet new responsibilities." This point-of-view was echoed among a number of lay members of the Governing Council who proposed the dismissal of some tenured staff on grounds of financial exigency. Similarly, the University administration was threatening the dismissal of some professional librarians as part of a massive cut in funding for the Robarts Library. What seemed a serious threat to tenure was effectively blocked, as Jean Smith pointed out to the Annual Spring Meeting of the Association, by the "frozen policies" clause in the Memorandum of Agreement.

In his report to the Spring Meeting and in a *Newsletter* that followed, Smith was cautiously optimistic about relations with the administration under the Memorandum of Agreement. He pointed to the effective grievance procedures that were now in place, to improved policies for sabbatical leave in some faculties, to improved salaries for librarians, to the "review of the entire rank structure ... for tutors and senior tutors" undertaken by the Joint Committee, and to the "positive change in the tone of campus dialogue" made possible by the Memorandum. At the same time, he admitted that the threat to dismiss librarians for reasons of financial exigency, along with the Governing Council's threat not to approve the Soberman Report, were worrisome. There was, he said, no guarantee under the Memorandum of Agreement against unfair bargaining practices—no recourse to the courts or the Labour Relations Board as under certification. On balance, however, Smith thought the first year under the Memorandum should be seen as "a modest success."

The following year the Faculty Association turned again to Dean Soberman as mediator/arbitrator in salary and benefit negotiations. Once again, his mediation having failed, Soberman was obliged to make an arbitral award. The across-the-board settlement he recommended, an increase of 5.4%, was slightly less disastrous in effect than his award the previous year; with the rate of inflation at just over 8%, it provided for a cut in real income of something under 3%.

But the tone of Soberman's second Report was oddly querulous. He complained that while fewer issues were outstanding than the year before, "both sides seemed to show more intransigence"; he had "serious reservations about the continued effectiveness of the current system"; he feared the gulf between the administration and the faculty, "certainly the faculty as represented by the Association," would continue to widen until serious negotiations became impossible. Most of all, Soberman seemed to find his joint role as mediator and arbitrator unworkable, his efforts at mediation eroded by the expectation on both sides of arbitration.

Jean Smith and the UTFA leadership were outraged by what Smith called the "gratuitous excesses" of Soberman's criticism of the Faculty Association. And, with a growing realization of the intractable decline of faculty salaries, a decline now of well over twenty per cent in real terms for the decade, the second Soberman award seemed somehow worse than the first, though it was, in fact, marginally better. At UTFA request, Dean Soberman's name was struck off the list of agreed mediator/arbitrators.

In the following year, 1980, with Michael Finlayson now the UTFA president, salary and benefit negotiations took a somewhat surprising turn. Finlayson and the Salary and Benefits Committee, supported by the Council, agreed to a settlement negotiated directly with the administration. This is the only time since salary discussions with the administration began in 1950 that the Association has agreed to a settlement neither imposed, nor mediated, nor arbitrated. It provided for an across-the-board salary increase of 8.0%, not as much an improvement over the previous two years as it seemed, since the rate of inflation was rising again towards one per cent per month. Both UTFA and the administration were anxious, however, to avoid the protracted and rancorous negotiations of the preceding year, and the UTFA negotiators, Soberman's awards fresh in their minds, decided they might do no better in arbitration than by agreeing to the administration's offer. In addition, Michael Finlayson thought he sensed a new collegiality in the administration's attitude towards UTFA.

By the following spring, however, the spring of 1981, the rise in the Consumer Price Index had attained an unprecedented velocity of more than thirteen per cent a year. The eight per cent agreed settlement of 1980 looked worse by the day. And what Michael Finlayson and Jim Conacher had agreed at the Spring Meeting in 1980 was the administration's new attitude of "brotherly love" was no longer perceptible. Once again the Association took salary and benefits negotiations to mediation; the new mediator/arbitrator was Professor Innis Christie of the Dalhousie Law Faculty.

Failing in mediation, Christie made a salary award of 9.1%, a figure essentially representing the University's administration's final position. Like Soberman, Christie complained at the confusion inherent in his dual role as mediator and arbitrator. Given the terms of the Memorandum of Agreement, he recommended more attention be paid to mediation since, if mediation failed, the mediator/arbitrator was not really free to act as an arbitrator at all. Under the existing system, Christie said, the arbitrator had to keep in mind that an award higher than the University administration's final offer would simply be rejected by the Governing Council.

There was considerable faculty indignation at the Christie award, as well as with Christie's frank admission that he felt he could not go above the University's final offer. Actually, Christie did UTFA, and Toronto faculty generally, a favour. He finally made clear, as Soberman had not done, the inherent weakness of the system of mediation/arbitration laid out in the Memorandum of Agreement. Jean Smith had argued that the formula agreed to in the Memorandum was effectively arbitration binding on both sides, since he thought the Governing Council could not reject an arbitrator's award without precipitating certification of a faculty union. But the fatal weakness in the formula was its inhibiting effect on the arbitrator who, in making his award, would not risk its rejection by the Governing Council. However useful in other respects the Memorandum of Agreement was, its provision for arbitration of salary and benefits disputes was illusory. In the first four years of negotiating under the terms of the Memorandum, faculty salaries had declined by about fifteen per cent in real terms, the steepest decline since that of the late 1940s.

Michael Finlayson abruptly abandoned his search for collegial negotiation with the administration and demanded amendment of the Memorandum to require binding arbitration in salary and benefit negotiations. The present formula, he said, was one of "binding supplication." He was supported by an UTFA Council resolution expressing outrage at the Christie award, and by a faculty-wide poll in which 86% of more than a thousand respondents endorsed the Council resolution and called for revision of Article VI in the Memorandum (minor revisions in the Memorandum in 1980 had redesignated Article IX, the original salary and benefits article, as Article VI).

Finlayson set up a special committee to consider various alternatives to Article VI as it stood. Without making a recommendation, the committee described these as ranging from doing nothing except to hope for a mediator who would "throw the long bomb"; to separating the mediator from the arbitrator, or seeking a fact-finder who would report without arbitral responsibility; to seeking binding arbitration; or, finally, seeking certification of a faculty union. Informal polls suggested a surprising willingness of Toronto faculty to engage in some kind of strike action. Advocates of such action pointed to the limited strike at York University that year where a certified faculty union had won a salary settlement substantially better than Toronto's. Suddenly the climate of faculty opinion at Toronto, heated by price inflation, had changed.

The UTFA Executive and Council had expected Adel Sedra, a member of the Executive from Electrical Engineering, to succeed Finlayson as UTFA President. Finlayson had asked Sedra to take the job, and Sedra had the support of most of the Executive. Presidential succession in the Association had always been by acclamation. But Harvey Dyck had decided that the time had come to press the administration on binding arbitration and thought that he himself was the best person for the job. Dyck was duly nominated to run against Sedra, and the Association had its first contested presidential election.

There was, in fact, little difference between Sedra and Dyck in principle, outlook, or plans for the Association. Some of their supporters saw Dyck as a more militant advocate of faculty power than Sedra, and saw Sedra, from an Engineering Department, as closer to the traditional caution of the professional faculties. Some members, especially from professional faculties, thought there had been a sufficient number of Association presidents from the History Department for a while (three, holding the office for six of the preceding ten years). But there was really no issue in the contest except perhaps, faintly, a perception of Sedra as an "inside" and Dyck as an "outside" candidate in respect to the current Executive and Council. It was a close election; Dyck won by a majority of eighteen votes out of nearly a thousand cast. Sedra agreed to remain on the Executive and was to be an effective and faithful supporter of Dyck and his policies.

Harvey Dyck probably had a wider and more comprehensive view of what the President of the Faculty Association ought to do, and might be able to do, than any of those who held the job before and after him. He saw his immediate task as getting a workable system of salary and benefits negotiations, but, beyond that, he wanted to use the negotiating power of the Toronto faculty to force the provincial government to increase university funding. He thought the time was right to try to reverse the university decline of the preceding decade. And there were signs of a moderation in the hostility towards universities that had characterized the attitude of the press, at least, during this time.

In the fall of 1981 *Maclean's* magazine published a revealing article on "The Crisis in the Universities," focusing on the state of Ontario universities, especially Toronto. The article pointed out that grant increases to universities in Ontario for the preceding six years had averaged only two-thirds those for other provinces, and that Ontario now ranked last among Canadian provinces in per capita spending for full-time students. The article provided abundant illustration of the impoverishment of the University of Toronto after a ten-year freeze on building renovation and the purchase of new equipment. The Department of Electrical Engineering needed $200,000 per year to maintain and replace equipment, and was getting $20,000. There were 50,000 titles in the Library awaiting processing, while 130 Library staff had recently been dismissed. The average $24,000 starting salary of assistant professors at Toronto was now less than that paid Toronto bus drivers. In what seemed to be a reviving public sympathy for the plight of the universities, Dyck thought he saw a glimmer of promise.

The chief obstacle, in Dyck's view, to a system of salary negotiations resolved by fair, independent, and binding arbitration, was the President of the University, Jim Ham. The faculty had generally welcomed Ham's appointment in 1978 when he succeeded John Evans.

An electrical engineer, Ham was personally popular, had served as Dean of Engineering and then as Dean of the Graduate School. In earlier times he had been active in the Faculty Association, and he was seen as a faculty person. As President, he was, however, to disappoint most Toronto faculty members. While conscientious, thoughtful, and straightforward, he seemed to many to be overwhelmed by the job. Rather than provide vigorous leadership in attempting, at least, to obtain acceptable funding for the University, he grimly accepted underfunding, immersed himself in detail, worked to achieve small economies, and tenaciously resisted increased expenditure. Before confronting him, Dyck made as careful an assessment as he could of Ham's outlook, and concluded he could never persuade him in argument to accept binding arbitration in salary settlements. Rather, he concluded, he would have to lay siege to Ham, deprive him of allies, and press him to the point where giving ground was his only option.

Beginning in the summer of 1981, Dyck methodically prepared his campaign. He could count, for the time being at least, on faculty support. Indignation over the Christie award had been fortified by the disparity between the 9% Toronto settlement and settlements elsewhere in Canada—12.1% at York, 12.5% at Calgary, 16.75% in the Quebec universities, and 18% in an arbitrator's award at the University of British Columbia.

To make the campaign for binding arbitration in a voluntary agreement effective, a willingness to consider certification of a faculty union was essential, and by October Dyck had a well-worked-out plan for certification in place. There was to be a skeleton coordinating committee of ten supervising a campaign to sign up union members, each member of the committee to be responsible for five or six Council constituencies. Jeffrey Sack had been asked to sketch out the probable limits of a bargaining unit, and the slight changes in the Constitution necessary to permit certification were ready to present to a general meeting. A new contract, based on the Memorandum of Agreement, could be drafted quickly.

An essential part of Dyck's preparations for negotiation was to assemble as much support for UTFA as he could from other University groups. This, of course, meant persuading others that the Faculty Association, in pursuing its own interests, could benefit the University as a whole. And here Dyck was effective in conveying his own breadth of vision on the plight of the University to other campus groups. The Faculty Association could, he argued, if it had binding arbitration in salary negotiations, lead an attack on underfunding that might well benefit not only other employees of the University, but students. He pressed this line of argument tirelessly, with the Staff Association, the teaching assistants' union, other campus unions, and, finally, with SAC, the main student organization. Relations with SAC had been cool, sometimes hostile, since the debate over a new Governing Act a decade earlier. But Dyck was able to get endorsement for UTFA's demands from SAC as well as from all the other principal campus groups. Prompt support from UTFA for the Library workers' union in its threatened strike helped solidify a sense of solidarity among these campus groups.

In seeking support from other University groups, Dyck did risk alienating conservative faculty members. When he announced UTFA support for the Library workers and distributed a SAC pamphlet in an UTFA mailing, a pamphlet which happened to contain an advertisement for an "all womens' dance," he provoked an outraged response from some UTFA members, especially from a group in the Chemistry Department. Adrian Brook, an intermittent critic of the Faculty Association for more than twenty years, finally resigned from the Association over its support for the Library workers. Brook's letter was somewhat intemperate, as was one from Bruce Bosnich and, especially, a letter from Peter Yates objecting to unions, strikes, and SAC, as well as to the advertisement of a dance for women only. Keith

Binding Arbitration

Yates also wrote a letter of protest, though it was more judiciously phrased than the others from his department. From Dyck's point-of-view the alienation of some conservative faculty members was unfortunate, but was an acceptable price to pay for university-wide support. University-wide, that is, with the exception of most members of the Governing Council and most senior academic administrators including the President.

In October the Governing Council agreed to consider revision of Article VI of the Memorandum. The UTFA Council approved a negotiating committee led by Harvey Dyck, its other members initially Jim Daniels, Diane Henderson from Library Science, Adel Sedra, and Kenneth Swinton from the Law Faculty. The administration agreed to December 8th as a deadline for negotiations, but was slow to begin serious talk. After preliminary discussion in which UTFA presented its demand for binding arbitration, the administration cancelled two meetings and presented no counter-proposal. Then, however, in late November in an action reminiscent of the negotiations five years earlier over the Memorandum, the Governing Council rejected UTFA's proposal as "misguided and irresponsible," and proposed its own formula for salary and benefit negotiations. This was simply that the Governing Council itself arbitrate a dispute between UTFA and the administration after mediation had failed. Dyck's negotiating team responded to this proposal with "dismay and disbelief" and rejected it out-of-hand.

The December 8th deadline was now only ten days away, and the pressure both on the administration and on the Faculty Association began to build up. Dyck had pressed ahead with plans for certification in the event negotiations to revise the Memorandum failed. Plans were made for a series of small meetings to be followed by a large meeting to revise the Constitution. The Executive Assistant, Victoria Grabb, who had been hired the year before by Michael Finlayson, took an active part in these preparations. She proposed that "front-line organizers" be trained to canvass members in the certification drive, and helped Dyck identify a group of dependable members to act as "poll captains." Growing support for certification was reported from Arts departments, from the librarians, and even from professional faculties. Adel Sedra found surprising support for certification from the Engineering Faculty, though some engineers were planning to seek a separate bargaining unit.

The Governing Council was reported to be deeply divided, some members resigned to faculty certification, others still hoping for compromise. Ham, under more and more pressure himself, was getting contrary advice from senior administrators and members of the Governing Council. One person whose advice he sought was uniquely qualified to comment on the issue at hand. This was Ernest Sirluck, like Ham a former Dean of the Graduate School, who had returned to Toronto after serving as President of the University of Manitoba at the time the faculty there did form a certified union. Ham asked Sirluck simply which was better, binding arbitration under the Memorandum of Agreement, or the prospect of arbitration after certification. Sirluck strongly advised the former on the grounds that, while a high arbitral award might do severe temporary damage to the University's financial position, it would not be irremediable damage, and the faculty would not be permanently severed from the senior academic administration as it would be in a certified union.

As the deadline approached and tension grew, the UTFA Executive and Council began to show signs of strain. Meetings were more and more frequent and protracted, and often held at inconvenient hours. At an early morning meeting of the Executive on the last day of November (the meeting began at 7:45 AM), Dyck tried to quiet discontent by urging members not to waver; "We all need good nerves," he said. Bill Graydon, an occasionally explosive engineer, resented Dyck's admonition and said he was tired of being bullied. Cecil Yip wondered whether the administration would really collapse;

Dyck reminded him that they had done so in 1977, and that it was no time to compromise or give an impression of weakness. Finally, on December 3rd, the administration gave ground. Ham authorized two vice-presidents, David Nowlan and Alex Pathy, to meet with Dyck and Adel Sedra to attempt to reach agreement on amending Article VI.

Real negotiations began on Sunday, December 6th, and were to continue for nine days, a week past the agreed deadline. At first, discussion seemed promising, and Ham appeared willing to accept binding arbitration in some form. But shortly serious differences appeared. Nowlan and Pathy argued for a time limit on any agreement, for a statement on the need for "fiscal responsibility" which would implicitly limit an arbitrator's freedom of action, and were adamant in opposing arbitration with "final offer selection," where the arbitrator would be obliged to choose between the final salary positions of the two sides. The UTFA negotiators eventually yielded on "final offer selection" (though this formula had worked successfully at other universities) and agreed to simple arbitration; and UTFA also agreed to a two-year trial with renewal only if mutually agreeable.

The most difficult question concerned a "fiscal responsibility" clause. Jeffrey Sack argued strenuously against agreeing to such a clause, however worded. He pointed out that "ability to pay" had been agreed not to be relevant in public sector arbitration, and that to agree to any limiting clause would simply legitimise a system that would guarantee ungenerous arbitral awards. Sack was supported in this view by Don Savage and Ron Levesque from CAUT, who were now taking an active role in advising UTFA.

Negotiations were broken off at 4:00 AM on Wednesday the 9th of December, but resumed two days later. Dyck was now under growing pressure to write off the negotiations and proceed to a certification drive. Jim Daniels and Adel Sedra worried that going beyond the original December 8th deadline would be seen by the administration as a sign of weakness. A number of members of the UTFA Executive and Council now supported immediate certification; Bill Graydon, Alan Horne, and Jim Daniels, among others, urged this course of action.

On Saturday, December 12th, the UTFA Council (which met four times in ten days) discussed the situation at length. Dyck put a motion before the Council to "undertake all measures necessary for certification while continuing to negotiate for a system of fair, independent and binding arbitration." Some Council members urged immediate certification; a number supported Dyck's motion; Stan Schiff urged caution. Only Jack Carr, a conservative economist, argued against proceeding with certification should negotiations fail. He objected to Jeffrey Sack's interventions and said that a decision to certify would be seen by the membership as "railroading"; why not continue under the present system for another year? In the event, the Council voted forty-one to one, with one abstention, in favour of Dyck's motion.

On Monday the 14th, Nowlan proposed new wording for criteria regarding salaries—"fair and reasonable" salaries linked to a requirement for the University to operate in a "responsible manner." Don Savage and Sack thought this no improvement, and Dyck seemed to agree. The Executive, however, was edging close to revolt. Graydon and Sedra wanted to disregard Sack's advice and accept the administration proposal. Cecil Yip agreed, and worried that if the proposal were to be rejected, the membership might refuse to support certification. Finally the Executive agreed to make a final effort to get all reference to salary criteria deleted but, if this proved impossible, to accept the administration proposal anyway. In a final session Dyck pressed the administration negotiators hard; surprisingly, perhaps because they had been impressed by the solid support for Dyck's motion at the Saturday meeting of the UTFA Council, they gave in, and agreed to eliminate all reference to salaries. On Tuesday the two sides signed an agreement, and on Wednesday, the 16th, Dyck brought the agreement before the Council.

There was some grumbling by a few Council members. Though Jeffrey Sack thought the agreement much improved, Derek Manchester opposed it and argued for certification, and Jack Wayne was dubious about its utility. But the Council approved the agreement by a vote of thirty-nine to two, with one abstention. Harvey Dyck, in a somewhat expansive mood, distributed thanks generously. He thanked the Council, the Executive, the negotiating committee, Adel Sedra, Cecil Yip, CAUT, Bill Nelson and Jean Smith, the Graduate Students' Union, the Staff Association, and Vicky Grabb. He and other Council members expressed much appreciation for Michael Finlayson's initial efforts in behalf of binding arbitration, and agreed to send him a telegram in Australia, where he was on leave, wishing him a Merry Christmas. Forgotten in this little celebration was the ominous two-year limitation written into the agreement.

There remained considerable opposition to the agreement inside the Governing Council. Despite Ham's endorsement, many members were prepared to vote against it. Eventually this opposition focussed on the question of whether the Governing Council had the power to give up its financial responsibilities under the Governing Act to an outside arbitrator. Jeffrey Sack, on behalf of UTFA, obtained two separate opinions unequivocally stating that the Governing Council, as a "natural person," had such a right; but the University lawyers thought perhaps not. In due course the Faculty Association and the Governing Council agreed to present this matter to the Supreme Court of Ontario as a "stated case." Finally, almost two years later, the Court ruled unsurprisingly that the Governing Council could indeed agree to outside arbitration of salary disputes.

In the meantime, the Governing Council having endorsed the agreement subject to any revision in future, the administration and the Faculty Association took up salary and benefit negotiations under the new Article VI. The agreed arbitrator was Kevin M. Burkett, second-in-command at the Ontario Labour Relations Board and an experienced and knowledgable arbitrator, though as Harvey Dyck warned, an arbitrator with "a reputation of being somewhat conservative in his awards." Failing in his mediative efforts, Burkett undertook to arbitrate the salary and benefits dispute between the University and the Faculty Association. His arbitration hearings took three days in early May, 1982, the Association represented by Jeffrey Sack. Burkett released his Report at the beginning of June.

The Burkett Report was a stunning endorsement of the Faculty Association's case on almost every issue. Burkett accepted the UTFA argument that Toronto faculty had suffered a 25% erosion of salaries between 1971 and 1981. He agreed that Toronto faculty salaries had lagged far behind those of other public sector employees and those of comparable professional people in private employment. He rejected the University administration's argument that progress-through-the-ranks increments should be taken into account in calculating the rate of salary increase, and accepted the UTFA argument that these were legitimately separate from, and formed no part of, salary increases.

Most important, Burkett ruled that the restoration of faculty salaries was a legitimate concern for the arbitrator, and that he was obliged to provide significant rectification of the Toronto salary scale. The faculty, he ruled, "should not be required to subsidize the community through substandard salaries." And, while recognizing the existence of fiscal restraints on the University's freedom of action, the goal of complete restoration of pre-1971 salary levels "must stand notwithstanding considerations of fiscal responsibility." "The equities," Burkett concluded, "weigh heavily in favour of the faculty." His award was an 18% across-the-board salary increase, plus the usual PTR increments, and, as well, improvements in vacation allowances and the PTR scheme for librarians, and an increase in sabbatical leave payments from 75% to 80% of salary.

Binding Arbitration

Some of Harvey Dyck's critics were later to argue that, with an increase in provincial funding of more than 12%, the University administration would have agreed to a salary settlement of, perhaps, 14% without binding arbitration. This is problematical and, in any event, misses the greater point—the importance of the Burkett Report in establishing the right of university faculty to restorative salary settlements. In the decade since it appeared, the Burkett Report has measurably strengthened the bargaining power of university faculty associations throughout Canada. It had an immediate echoing effect on other Ontario settlements in 1982 and, indeed, on salary settlements for non-academic staff at Toronto and elsewhere. Burkett, incidentally, devised a means of introducing the awarded salary increase over nine months in a series of three increments, in order to reduce the immediate burden on the University salary budget to about 12%. Because of the high rate of inflation at the time, Burkett's 18% award included only 6% or so in restorative salary, leaving about 18% for future "catch-up" awards by, presumably, future arbitrators.

After Harvey Dyck had presented the terms of the Burkett Report to a Faculty Association Council meeting, he was given a rousing round of applause. There was no question in anyone's mind of Dyck's central and dominant role in forcing "fair, independent, and binding arbitration" on an unwilling administration and a hostile Governing Council. Whether someone else might have achieved the same result that year is an unanswerable question. What is certain is the skill and sureness with which Dyck had handled negotiations. There were those, it is true, who found him overbearing at times, and, though he was meticulous in seeking advice, some felt he had usually made up his mind before consulting anyone. Had his efforts failed, Dyck would have taken much of the blame. But they did not fail, and throughout this difficult time, he kept his confidence in himself and in the certainty of the other side yielding if pushed hard enough. At heart, Dyck was apprehensive of certification, but he nevertheless made the threat of certification more credible, both to faculty and the administration, than it had ever been.

It is tempting to compare Harvey Dyck with Jean Smith, the other Faculty Association president who forced the administration to yield much more than it wished to do. Smith, though he had been a professional soldier for some years in his youth, was diplomatic, senatorial, and persuasive. His style was quietly to make a case that it seemed uncivil and unreasonable to deny. It was Dyck whose methods were military. He was remorseless in seeking out and attacking the enemy's weaknesses. He was, somewhat improbably, a Mennonite warrior.

Of course, both Smith and Dyck left serious questions unresolved: Smith, the matter of a workable system of collective bargaining; Dyck, the problem of what would happen once the two-year trial of binding arbitration was over. Some still think that a straightforward collective bargaining agreement reached by a faculty union certified under the provincial labour laws would have been more in the interest of Toronto faculty than either Smith's Memorandum or Dyck's try at collective bargaining. But perhaps to think this is only to wish that the University of Toronto were a different place and its faculty of a different temperament.

Chapter Eight
Revision And Retreat

There was to be a confused and disappointing sequel to what had seemed to be the establishment in 1982 of binding arbitration in salary and benefits disputes. In agreeing to a two-year trial period, Harvey Dyck, as well as most others active in the Association at the time, had assumed that, once in place, binding arbitration could not be repudiated by the Governing Council without precipitating the certification of a faculty union. The validity of this assumption was undermined by a series of events.

In September, 1982 the Provincial government, alarmed by a series of high salary settlements, among which the Burkett Award was itself significant, put through a *Wage Restraint Act*, limiting salary increases for employees in the public service, including those in universities, to five per cent for the following year. The Act did not affect the Burkett settlement, but it precluded salary negotiations the following year. For 1983-84 the imposed salary settlement at Toronto was just under five per cent.

The rate of inflation fell sharply in the latter part of 1983 and 1984 to an average annual rate of about 4.5% at which it was to remain for the rest of the decade. Wage restraint legislation was not extended, and salary and benefit negotiations were again in prospect in the fall of 1983. These were delayed, however, initially by both sides waiting for the Ontario Supreme Court's decision on the "stated case." When the Supreme Court finally ruled that it was indeed legal for the University to enter into an agreement providing for binding arbitration of salary disputes, the Governing Council in January, 1984, belatedly ratified the revised Article VI.

Far from settling the question of binding arbitration, the Governing Council's action led immediately to a renewal of the whole debate over collective bargaining. And it shortly became clear that a primary obstacle to binding arbitration was the President of the University, David Strangway. Strangway's presidency was itself tragically accidental. At the expiration of Ham's term of office, the presidency had been offered to Donald Forster, who had accepted. Forster had been President of the University of Guelph since 1975, but earlier had had considerable administrative experience at Toronto. He had served as an assistant to Claude Bissell and later as Provost under John Evans. Although he had, more often than not, dealt with the Faculty Association as an adversary, Don Forster was held in high regard by most faculty members who had known him. He knew the University well; he had a quick and discriminating mind; he could be both decisive and judicious; and he was usually good-humoured and cool-tempered. But at the end of the summer in 1983, a few days before he was to take up his presidential duties at Toronto, Forster died suddenly of a heart attack. Strangway, the Provost, was offered the presidency for 1983-84 while the search for a full-term President was renewed. Strangway accepted this appointment provided he be named "President," not "Acting President," and he was himself an active candidate for the regular appointment.

Of all the Toronto presidents with whom the Faculty Association has had to deal, Strangway was probably the most unsympathetic. He was almost contemptuously unafraid of faculty certification; strikes and lockouts, he said, were better than arbitration. At the same time, Strangway could be plausible in argument and agreeable in manner. Having induced the Governing Council to resolve to consider anew the whole matter of salary and benefit negotiations with the Faculty Association, Strangway approached the UTFA President, Cecil Yip, and asked his endorsement for a new approach. Yip had succeeded Harvey Dyck as President in the summer of 1983. A distinguished medical researcher from Banting and Best, he had served the Faculty Association well for some years. He had chaired the UTFA Grievance Committee and served on the Academic Freedom and Tenure Committee of CAUT. As Vice-President and a useful member of Harvey Dyck's Executive, he was a natural choice to succeed Dyck.

As a former Grievance chair, Yip was used to negotiating with the University administration. Grievance negotiations were sometimes adversarial but, being within the terms of an agreed and defined structure, seldom confrontational. Yip himself disliked confrontation and had a genuinely collegial attitude towards faculty and administration alike. When asked by Strangway to endorse a fresh approach to collective bargaining negotiations, Yip agreed. He was later to argue with perfect sincerity that he was merely endorsing the principle of collegial negotiation, not modifying the Faculty Association's position on any issue. Strangway and the Governing Council, however, used Yip's endorsement to argue that the form of salary negotiation was once again an open question, that the "slate had been wiped clean."

The state of faculty association negotiations with the administration was put in further doubt by a dispute over whether there remained, or did not remain, a second year of Dyck's agreement permitting binding arbitration. The Association argued that, as wage restraint legislation had prevented any negotiations for 1983-84 benefits, there was still a year remaining of Dyck's two-year agreement, and negotiations for 1984-85 should be carried on with the possibility of an arbitrated settlement. The administration and Governing Council argued that the two-year term of Dyck's agreement had expired, and cited Yip's endorsement of new negotiations as implicit support for this view. Yip argued that he had neither abandoned the second year of Dyck's agreement nor the Association's commitment to binding arbitration, but the Faculty Association now found itself on the defensive.

Through the late winter and spring of 1984, Michael Donnelly, chairing the UTFA Salary and Benefits Committee, carried on fruitless and frustrating discussion with the administration, represented usually by Frank Iacobucci, now the Provost. At a March Council meeting, Cecil Yip spoke of the need for patience and good faith in these negotiations. Stan Schiff abruptly rejected this advice. Iacobucci, he said, was smart, skilled, and stalling. To talk of "good faith" was foolish. The administration, Schiff said, was no longer afraid of faculty certification, and he wished Harvey Dyck was leading UTFA. When Yip objected to this implied reproach, Schiff said he had meant no offence, but that Harvey Dyck had been "a phenomenon." The Council eventually reaffirmed support for binding arbitration in a voluntary agreement, and for certification if this was not agreed to by the Governing Council.

These resolutions were taken to a well-attended, but not wholly harmonious, General Meeting in April. Donnelly described the stone wall he had run into in his discussions with Iacobucci. The administration had chastised the Faculty Association for trying to set pre-conditions in these discussions, had flatly refused to discuss the revisions of Article VI that had been made in Dyck's agreement, and had dismissed this agreement as a "quick fix for a dirty deal." The administration's own offer was a cloudy proposal for putting both sides' positions in a salary dispute before the "University community," but with no provision for resolving an impasse.

Some faculty conservatives intervened vigorously in the debate. Mike Uzumeri said he still supported the demand for binding arbitration, but not the proposal to seek certification of a faculty union should negotiations fail. Art Kruger and Noah Meltz thought the administration's proposals were worth considering. John Crispo was full of alarm: a certification drive, he said, might fail; if it succeeded, the faculty might refuse to strike; if there were a strike, it might be lost; in bargaining after certification, "tenure might be on the line." Finally, however, the meeting passed both resolutions: to continue to seek binding arbitration in a voluntary agreement; and to seek certification if binding arbitration could not be obtained.

Thus it was a revived and obdurate administration and a more-than-usually hostile Governing Council that the new UTFA President and Executive faced in the summer of 1984. Harvey Dyck, it turned out, had wounded but not slain the dragon of Simcoe Hall paternalism. The new UTFA President was Peter Dyson, the only member from the English Department ever to hold this office. It was perhaps both Dyson's and the Association's misfortune that he did not come to the UTFA presidency a little later. His real interest lay in the equity issues that later in the 1980s were to dominate Association activities. He had been a sensitive, dedicated, and efficient chairman of the Grievance Committee, and was used, like Cecil Yip, to dealing with the administration adversarially but within agreed rules. Like Yip, Dyson disliked confrontation, but he and his Executive undertook to make the best they could of the situation they found themselves in.

For the Faculty Association, the prospects in the summer and fall of 1984 were considerably less promising than they had been three years before. Then, Harvey Dyck's campaign for binding arbitration had been fuelled by faculty frustration and outrage at the end of a decade of rapidly falling real income, and at a time of 13% annual inflation. But the Burkett Award itself had taken the edge off the faculty's salary discontent, and the rate of inflation had fallen to under 5%. Guided by Frank Iacobucci, the administration was managing its case with far more skill than in Harvey Dyck's or Jean Smith's time. And the threat of faculty certification, used so effectively in 1976 by Smith and in 1981 by Dyck, had lost credibility. The administration did not think a complacent and aging faculty would certify, and cared less than in earlier times whether it did or not. So Dyson and his Executive felt, perhaps rightly, that they could not hold straightforwardly to a demand for binding arbitration, and if they failed to obtain it, go directly to certification. It was a realistic sense of a weakened bargaining position that led Dyson and his Executive to consider alternative courses of action.

During the summer and fall of 1984 Dyson and the Executive struggled to find a way to outflank the administration. Increasingly Vicky Grabb, the Executive Assistant, dominated negotiations, although her proposals were always correctly made to, and approved by, the Executive. Grabb had worked effectively with Harvey Dyck and had had considerable experience in labour and political organization. Her proposals were persuasive and often ingenious, but taken cumulatively, they created a sense of shifting positions that confused the faculty and sometimes increased the appearance of weakness they were designed to overcome.

At one point the Association made a "conditional offer" to the administration of arbitration by a wholly neutral panel whose recommendations could be rejected by either side. Later the Association put forward a woefully cumbersome set of alternative proposals which further obscured the clarity of the original stand on binding arbitration. Finally, in October, the Executive set about seriously organizing faculty support for a certification drive. By this time many ordinary members of the Association were thoroughly perplexed. One member of Dyson's Executive, Jim Estes, resigned in October, complaining of Vicky Grabb's domination of negotiations and of the Executive's lack of political judgment.

There was growing criticism of the Executive in the Council, especially from Harvey Dyck who came as a guest. Dyck behaved rather like a general who had left his forces nicely disposed in a strong position, and had come back to find them in disarray, their position abandoned. Although his specific criticisms often made sense, the relentless ferocity of his attacks on the Executive added to the sense of indirection and floundering that many loyal supporters of the Association now felt. Dyck castigated the Executive for blunders and poor judgment; he denounced the "conditional offer"; he complained at the lack of effective communication from the Executive to the membership; the Executive's arguments, he said, were "childlike in their simplicity." Dyck had been at his best in 1981 when he was in charge and dealing from a position of strength. Now, frustrated by the weakened position of the Association and his own inability to do much about it, he turned his considerable powers of attack, used so effectively against the administration in 1981, against Dyson and his Executive.

One impediment to serious negotiation with the administration had, however, been removed. Strangway had not been chosen for a full-term presidency. Rather, that appointment had gone to George Connell, a biochemist who had been at Toronto for many years and had served in John Evans's administration before taking the presidency of the University of Western Ontario.

In early November, Iacobucci agreed to resume negotiations with Donnelly, and, within a few days, the two sides agreed to a new revision of Article VI. This provided sensibly for mediation and arbitration to be separate, removing the old duality of the mediator/arbitrator's role. Less happily it proposed an odd compromise on the question of binding arbitration, a compromise suggested by Iacobucci and the University lawyers: in a given year, the Governing Council might reject an arbitrator's award; if it did so, however, there would be conventional binding arbitration the following year.

Dyson and Donnelly brought the new proposal to the UTFA Council on November 15th. Dyck, again attending as a guest, thought the proposal seriously flawed: it should not have been agreed to; certification would have been better; there would now be no way seriously to influence the funding policies of the Provincial government; it was "a sad day for the Association." Adel Sedra agreed, suggesting that a repudiated award one year might well be followed by a very modest binding settlement the next. Derek Manchester argued for continuing the certification drive. Jeffrey Sack, however, defended the agreement as workable, even if not as strong as straight binding arbitration. Stan Schiff thought the agreement made certification now impractical. Other members spoke in favour of the agreement—Peter Fitting, Fred Wilson, Nanda Choudhry, Cecil Yip. Eventually the Council endorsed the agreement, agreed to cancel the proposed Membership Meeting meant to launch a certification drive, as well as a faculty referendum, preliminary results of which had shown 60% support for certification.

The Governing Council ratified the new Article VI, and salary negotiations for 1984-85 and 1985-86 got under way, mediated eventually by Martin Teplitsky. Both sides were to accept the settlement he proposed, a "temporizing settlement," he called it—an across-the-board salary increase of 3.3% for 1984-85, and 3.2% for 1985-86; these represented an increase of 1.7% below the rate of inflation for the two years.

Teplitsky was to mediate successfully two later two-year settlements, and only once have negotiations under the re-revised Article VI gone to arbitration. This was in 1986 when the arbitrator was Donald Munroe, former Chairman of the British Columbia Labour Relations Board. Munroe reaffirmed the Burkett principle of salary restoration, but his award was disappointing to the Association—6.5% across-the-board, 2.0% of which was for restoration of lost income. The two per cent "catch-up," in fact, roughly equalled the loss in real income *since* the Burkett settlement, leaving intact the eighteen per cent still owing the faculty under Burkett's formula.

Although the Governing Council grudgingly approved the Munroe Award, President Connell outraged faculty opinion and gave needless comfort to those in the Provincial government opposed to increased university funding by complaining that the settlement was too high.

Curiously, neither at the time of the Munroe Award nor earlier when the 1984 revision of Article VI was being considered, did critics of the alternate-year scheme of arbitration seem to grasp what may be its most serious weakness: this is not what might or might not happen after the Governing Council rejected an arbitral award. Rather it is the unlikelihood of an arbitrator making an award the Governing Council would be tempted to reject. Although they have more latitude because the Governing Council must worry about arbitration the following year, arbitrators under the present system are in somewhat the position of Soberman and Christie under the original Memorandum. Wishing their awards to be accepted, they are unlikely to press too hard the side holding the power of rejection.

During the contentious debate within the Association in the fall of 1984, the Executive became concerned at criticism of Vicky Grabb and the vulnerability of her position as Executive Assistant of the Association. Peter Dyson agreed to a "staff employment contract" providing for possible arbitration of any dismissal of the Executive Assistant or the Administrative Assistant, Sue Ann Elite; it also provided "permanent status" to both officers; and provided for one year's salary, plus one month's salary for each year of service, to the Executive Assistant in case of dismissal, and for six month's salary, plus two weeks' salary for each year of service, to the Administrative Assistant in case of dismissal. Dyson signed contracts embodying these terms, and put the matter before the Council.

The problem Dyson addressed here is, of course, inherent in the staff relations of any organization, public or private, where a transient and amateur controlling body deals with the organization's permanent employees. Diana Moeser, the Faculty Association's first Executive Assistant, a strong-willed and able person, had been summarily dismissed by Jean Smith in 1977, essentially because Smith felt there was room in the UTFA office for only one voice of authority. Moeser had accepted a modest settlement mediated by an ad hoc committee of Council. At OCUFA there had been more than one clash between permanent staff members and the Executive. Dyson, however, in attempting with entire goodwill to protect Vicky Grabb, seemed to some members of Council to have gone too far on his own.

The Council referred the matter of staff contracts to a committee, and the affair remained unsettled until the spring of 1985 when Vicky Grabb resigned to take a position with the Education Relations Commission. When Dyson reported her resignation to Council, he praised her work with the Association and said she had professionalized the Executive Assistant's job. Anyone comparing the records and methods of the Association before Grabb's time with those during and since her tenure must agree.

Underneath the criticism of Dyson and his Executive with respect to their negotiations with the administration, and then with regard to the staff contracts, a more fundamental division of view about the management of the Association became evident in 1984 and 1985. This would very likely have been the case whoever was President, whoever was Executive Assistant, and whoever the members of the Executive. The fact was, the Association had changed and was changing. The Memorandum of Agreement had given contractual form to relations with the administration which had previously been casual. Both the grievance work handled by the Association and benefits negotiations now required more work, time, and professional competence than in the past. A group of new issues, or old issues newly considered, was, or was about to be, added to the Association's range of activities—issues regarding the status of women, consideration of a Sexual Harassment Code, proposals for changes in academic appointment procedures. Some of this new burden of work fell on the permanent staff, but a good deal of it was adding to the work of the Executive. The Association President had had half released time since

144

1971, but now the Grievance and Salary and Benefits chairs had one-quarter released time. To a limited degree, the running of the Faculty Association was not only becoming professional for the permanent staff, but semi-professional for members of the Executive.

Among rank-and-file members of the Association who took an interest in its activities, and especially among people who had been active in the Association in the past, there was a bias towards the amateurism of earlier times. One objection to certification of a faculty union had always been the prospect of a union bureaucracy replacing the informal senior faculty management of the old Association. The prominent role Vicky Grabb had come to play in shaping Association policy, and the apparent willingness of Dyson and his Executive to endorse this role and give it permanence provoked a reaction.

Early in 1985 Harvey Dyck discussed his concerns about the direction of the Association with Jean Smith who, in general, shared these concerns. Smith spoke to me about this, and I to Michael Finlayson. The four of us, claiming, I suppose, some legitimacy as recent former presidents of the Association, met a few times, and finally had a meeting with Peter Dyson and some members of his Executive. Dyck was, as usual, forthright in his criticisms, the rest of us supporting him in varying degree. Eventually the rest of what I called "The Gang of Four" persuaded Michael Finlayson to run for the UTFA presidency for 1985-86. Finlayson set one condition, that his nomination form be signed by a majority of Council members. This condition was met; Dyson decided not to contest Finlayson's election, and Finlayson was acclaimed President. He then persuaded Harvey Dyck to accept nomination as Salary and Benefits chair, and this provoked a revolt among some Council members. Jack Wayne, who had had considerable experience in UTFA affairs and had served on Cecil Yip's Executive, was also nominated, and the Council had to decide between him and Dyck.

The debate focussed almost entirely on Harvey Dyck. Dyck's critics included Wayne himself, Dyson, and Michael Donnelly, supported by Bruce Kidd, Peter Fitting, and Cecil Yip. Dyck, they claimed, was divisive, confrontational, and too much given to acting on his own. Dyck was strongly supported, however, by a number of others—Michael Finlayson, Adel Sedra, Stan Schiff, Nanda Choudhry, Jim Estes, Bill Dick, and Derek Manchester. Essentially, their argument was that Dyck was best qualified to negotiate with the administration *because* he was tough and confrontational. Derek Manchester said wryly "that although he knew Professor Dyck well, he would support him for the position." Participants in this debate divided evenly between Dyck's supporters and his opponents. But when the Council voted, its silent majority, stung by Dyck's bitter speeches and mindful of Dyson's and his Executive's efforts in difficult circumstances, supported Wayne by a vote of twenty-nine to fourteen with one abstention.

Under Michael Finlayson's second presidency, from 1985 to 1987, the trend towards the professionalization of Faculty Association activities was not reversed; indeed, if anything, its pace accelerated. Most of the members of Finlayson's Executive had either served with Peter Dyson or had supported him. The two people who have held the presidency of the Association since Finlayson's term ended were both members of Dyson's Executive.

Collective bargaining, while remaining a central activity of the Association, has lost the intensity of focus it had before 1985. Except for the Munroe Award in 1986, all the salary and benefit settlements of recent years have been in the form of two-year mediated settlements, those of 1987-89 and 1989-91 mediated by Teplitsky, and that of 1991-93 by John McCamus, an economist at York University. The across-the-board settlements between 1987 and 1992 averaged 4.9%, while the rate of inflation in these years averaged about 4.4%. If the agreed 4.0% settlement for 1992-93 is taken into account (with the rate of inflation at less than two per cent), the faculty has, in fact, achieved a salary "catch-up" in recent years of close to four per cent.

As long as UTFA was confronting the University administration on the issue of collective bargaining and, especially, as long as the Toronto association was seriously considering certification of a faculty bargaining unit as in 1981 and again in 1984, relations with CAUT were fairly close. As the emphasis on collective bargaining waned, and the prospect of certification grew more remote, discontent with CAUT increased. From the early 1970s on, CAUT had been heavily engaged in supporting certified associations, and its staff and expenses had increased sharply. Some local associations which had not certified found CAUT's dues more and more burdensome, and its services increasingly unhelpful.

By 1986, of total income from dues of $500,000, UTFA was paying CAUT $170,000, or 34% (compared with $105,000, or 21%, to OCUFA). When Michael Finlayson asked CAUT to contribute $30,000 to the cost of Munroe's arbitration, CAUT offered only $15,000, even though the Munroe Award had considerably influenced other University settlements. In September, 1986, Finlayson arranged a meeting in Winnipeg of delegates from a number of faculty associations to consider what reforms in CAUT's structure might be proposed, and how the burden of CAUT dues might be reduced. The Alberta and Saskatchewan associations had already withdrawn from CAUT, and several other large associations shared Finlayson's concern, but most delegates to the Winnipeg meeting supported CAUT, and no agreement was reached.

When, in the winter of 1986-87, it appeared that CAUT was unwilling to take any serious steps to respond to criticism from UTFA and from other like-minded associations, Finlayson persuaded the Executive and Council to give notice to CAUT of Toronto's withdrawal at the end of the academic year. Associations at Carleton and the University of Western Ontario took similar action.

147

CAUT did respond to these harsh steps, setting up an ad hoc committee of representatives from major faculty associations to advise on reforms. This committee proposed, and the CAUT Council accepted, major changes in the national Association's funding and operations. Management was simplified by the elimination of the old Board, staff was cut, and CAUT's functions were divided into its traditional activities of lobbying and the defence of academic freedom and tenure on the one hand and collective bargaining services on the other. Eventually a Collective Bargaining Cooperative was established, whose services individual faculty associations could subscribe to and pay for, but which associations need not join. For those associations, Toronto included, which did not join the Cooperative, dues were sharply reduced. Toronto's dues fell by a third over three years.

Although Finlayson and his Executive were satisfied with these reforms, and withdrew the proposal to leave CAUT, there was criticism from some UTFA members of Finlayson's actions in dealing with CAUT. He was accused of being unnecessarily brutal and uncollegial. It was pointed out that, expressed as a mill rate, CAUT dues had not risen in a decade; that the CAUT's staff had grown in the early 1970s, but not since; that payments to CAUT, as a percentage of UTFA's income, had not risen in recent years, and had actually fallen over a longer time.

At the Annual Meeting in April, 1987, a number of members, led by Chandler Davis and Harvey Dyck, defended CAUT, pointing to its historical role in defense of academic freedom in Canada and its many services to the Toronto Association in the past. Dyck recalled the valuable help Don Savage and Ron Levesque had given UTFA at the time the binding arbitration agreement was being negotiated, and the substantial financial support CAUT had then pledged UTFA, in case of need. Other members, Finlayson himself, Paul Thompson, and Stan Schiff, defended the harsh treatment of CAUT as justified and effective, pointing to CAUT's self-reformation as healthy and as unlikely to have been achieved without severe pressure.

Relations between UTFA and CAUT were to remain cool for a time, but Fred Wilson who succeeded Finlayson as President, gradually achieved a renewed working relationship. In the meantime, UTFA's relations with OCUFA have been placid, especially as OCUFA's lobbying activities with the Provincial government seemed in the 1980s to become more sophisticated and productive. By 1992 Toronto's CAUT and OCUFA dues combined, expressed as a mill rate, were almost exactly what they had been fifteen years before, though the OCUFA proportion had risen a little and the CAUT proportion fallen. And in 1991-92, for the first time, the presidents of both CAUT and OCUFA were from Toronto, Fred Wilson at CAUT and Bill Graham at OCUFA.

Chapter Nine
Different Times

Assessing the role of the faculty association at Toronto during the past decade is, in one way, like trying to give an intelligible account of its activities in the 1940s. Both decades are in shadow, though for very different reasons. For the 1940s there is little surviving evidence and few memories. For the most recent decade, there is an abundance of material evidence, written and oral, but events are too close to judge with any sureness, and many matters are unfinished and uncertain in outcome.

It is evident, however, that early in the 1980s the emphasis and direction of Faculty Association activities began to change. Even while collective bargaining was still at the centre of UTFA activities, as it was until 1985, new people with new concerns were becoming active in the direction of the Association. If the 1950s were dominated by salary and benefits matters, rather narrowly considered, and the 1960s by the question of university government, and the 1970s by the drive for effective collective bargaining, the most recent decade has seen an increasing focus on equity issues. The Association has paid more and more attention, with uneven results, to the interests of the most vulnerable and marginal members of the faculty community— grievors, women, pensioners and aging faculty, non-tenured faculty, especially tutors.

Vicky Grabb left the Faculty Association in May, 1985, and in June, her successor, Suzie Scott began work. Suzie Scott was an American with a law degree from Toronto and six years' experience as a defence lawyer. She has now worked for the Association for seven years, her position as a lawyer providing clear benefits to her and to UTFA. As a lawyer, she has not had to define her professional identity solely in terms of her position in the Faculty Association. She has also frequently been able to give the Association legal advice for which it otherwise would have had to pay outsiders. Finally, the equity issues and grievances that have been at the centre of Association activities in recent years have been well-suited to her experience and temperament.

Negotiations for, ultimate agreement on, and recent revisions of the University's Sexual Harassment Policy have been a particular concern of Suzie Scott's. The perceived need for such a policy, at Toronto and elsewhere, arose a decade ago, initially in response to demands from women's rights groups. CAUT issued guidelines on the subject in 1982 and that year an ad hoc University group calling itself the Sexual Harassment Coalition was formed. The UTFA Grievance Committee had informal discussions with the Coalition beginning in 1982, as did the University administration.

Once the administration agreed to implement a formal policy, the Association argued that its agreement to any such policy was required under Article II of the Memorandum, since a code on sexual harassment implicitly affected staff policies and procedures already in effect. After much negotiation and discussion with a wide variety of campus groups, agreement was reached on a code in 1987, its actual drafting in the hands of David Cook, the Vice-Provost, and Suzie Scott. The form and language of the code, properly the Sexual Harassment Policy, was mainly provided by Scott whose commitment to women's rights, but even more to individual rights, fitted nicely the Faculty Association's concern to balance the rights and interests of members who might be either accusers or accused.

Since 1986 UTFA has had a Committee on the Status of Women, chaired first by Helen Rosenthal and, more recently, by Rhonda Love.

Two issues have been at the centre of this Committee's work. One has been difficult and laborious to resolve, but not essentially controversial. This has been the matter of women's equity in salary and other conditions of employment. Here the Faculty Association has generally had the support of the University administration. Since the passage of the *Pay Equity Act* in 1987, the University has been obliged by law to identify and correct salary inequities inherent in occupations dominated by females. This has meant finding male-dominated groups of employees that can be compared with female-dominated groups doing work of similar skill, and correcting inequities specific to groups. Additionally the University, in order to be able to bid on a range of federally funded research projects, has been obliged to seek out and correct *individual* inequities.

For several years a Female Faculty Salary Review has been in process, extending throughout the University, department by department and faculty by faculty. Recommendations from chairs and deans have gone to a committee chaired by David Cook, on which UTFA has been represented by Rhonda Love and Suzie Scott. This Review has been nearly completed; hundreds of individual cases have been considered and many increases in salary have been made, ranging from small amounts to as much, in one case, as $24,000 annual salary. These adjustments have been substantial in total, adding about a million dollars to the faculty salary budget.

The other main issue raised by the Status of Women Committee has been the controversial matter of preferential hiring of women for faculty positions. This issue is analagous in some respects to the question of Canadianization in the 1970s and, as that issue did, has divided the faculty along lines often different from lines of division on other issues.

On the urging of the Status of Women Committee, supported by the Executive, the UTFA Council endorsed a formula in support of preferential hiring in 1987. In its final form it provided that when

153

"one sex is under-represented in the hiring department, and the qualifications of a candidate of the other sex are not demonstrably better
than the qualifications of the best candidate of the under-represented
sex, then the candidate of the under-represented sex shall be recommended for the position." There has been considerable argument over
what "demonstrably better" means, over whether any non-academic
criterion is justifiable in making academic appointments, and over
whether traditional academic criteria actually are objective. Some
strong supporters of the Faculty Association have refused to endorse
any formula for preferential hiring of women. Stan Schiff, for example, after seventeen years on the Council, left over this issue.

The rights of aging and retired faculty members have constituted
another equity issue of recent years. When Section 15 of the Charter
of Rights came into effect in the spring of 1985, it appeared that
University enforcement of mandatory retirement on the basis of age
might violate the provisions of the Charter. CAUT decided to support
an appeal against mandatory retirement by a number of faculty members and librarians at several Ontario universities, including Toronto.
This appeal eventually made its way to the Supreme Court of Canada,
which issued its decision in December, 1990, more than five years
after the initial court action.

As late as the day before the ruling was made public, the Toronto
media expected a decision favourable to the appellants, and one of the
University's lawyers was offering bets that the University would "lose"
the case, that is, that mandatory retirement would be struck down.
The Court, however, had taken an increasingly narrow view of Charter "rights," a view deferential both to business interests and government. In the event, the majority of the Court ruled that, while
mandatory retirement on grounds of age did indeed violate the Charter of Rights, the violation did not justify judicial intervention.

As so frequently in the past, the Toronto faculty association had
lagged behind CAUT on this issue. When Hank Rogers, the Griev-

ance Chair, first reported to the membership on mandatory retirement in 1985, he was carefully neutral in his comments. As President
of UTFA, Michael Finlayson, however, strongly endorsed the CAUT
position and persuaded the Council to pass a resolution opposing
mandatory retirement and urging a flexible retirement policy on the
administration.

Of course, for seventeen years, from 1955 to 1972, the Toronto
retirement age had been 68, abruptly lowered to 65 in 1972 without
consultation with UTFA. A few years later the "frozen policies" clause
in the Memorandum would have made such a unilateral change impossible. As it is, Toronto remains one of the very few major universities in North America with mandatory retirement at 65 and,
consequently, lacks inducement to provide the flexible retirement
plans which now characterize most universities.

Pensions are an old, almost an original, faculty association interest
at Toronto, antedating even concern over salaries. As mentioned earlier in this account, the present pension plan dates from 1966, though
it has been considerably modified. As was the case with earlier plans,
however, the benefits of the present plan have been eroded by inflation. Until the 1980s pension payments were increased haphazardly
by percentages ranging from close to the rate of inflation to as much
as 6% below it. In the days of high inflation in the early 1980s, a
rule-of-thumb policy was adopted, that the rate of increase should
equal the rate of inflation minus 4%. This formula made it likely that
pension income would lose half its purchasing power over a decade.

In 1987 Michael Finlayson negotiated an agreement by which the
Association gave up any claims to an accumulated pension surplus (or
liability to a deficit) in exchange for an annual increase representing
60% of the increase in the Consumer Price Index, or that rate of
increase minus 4%, whichever was greater. This agreement did reduce
the rate of erosion in the value of pensions, but it was based on

actuarial estimates that grossly underestimated the accumulating surplus in the pension plan.

The question of how forthcoming the administration was in providing the Association with actuarial information at the time of the 60% agreement is still contentious, the Association arguing that actuarial estimates were radically changed immediately after the agreement was made, the administration maintaining that the Association simply did not understand all the information it was given during negotiations. The essential point is, of course, that the pension plan has produced a greater and greater surplus, not because of wise management on the part of the University, but because of the same inflationary forces that have eaten away at the real value of pensions. Thus, since the 1987 agreement, the University has built up "Long Term Adjustment" and Endowment funds of something over one hundred twenty million dollars with money that had been earmarked to meet the legal obligations of funding the pension plan but was surplus to those obligations. In addition, the University administration has diverted to other purposes monies originally intended for funding pensions, a practice that goes back at least until 1980.

In 1991 UTFA and the administration agreed to a raise in the indexation of pensions from 60% to 75%, a significant improvement, though the case for full indexation of faculty pensions is strong. The argument is sometimes made that Toronto faculty do not have as good a claim to fully indexed pensions as, say, civil servants or Ontario teachers, because the faculty contribution to the plan, 5% of salary, now raised to 6%, is significantly below the 9% contribution of most groups that do have full indexation. This argument is false, however, since, over the years, the Faculty Association has achieved such improvements in the pension plan as have been made, by accepting reduced salary settlements. Foregone salary, in fact, represents enough to bring the real pension contribution of faculty members to about 9% annually. The moral claim of retired Toronto faculty to substantial

156

restoration of the purchasing power of their pensions is very strong. To what degree this may also constitute a legal claim remains to be tested.

A final major equity issue in recent years concerns proposed changes in academic categories, and appointments policies and procedures. In 1985 the University administration proposed some changes in University appointments policy that, falling under the "frozen policies" clause in the Memorandum of Agreement, required UTFA's agreement. Faculty association representatives entered into protracted discussion with the administration culminating in the spring of 1987 with what UTFA thought was a negotiated agreement with the administration. In the fall of 1987, however, the Provost, Joan Foley, disavowed this agreement, arguing that there had been no "negotiations," but only preliminary discussion, and that she would have to seek further advice within the administration.

The UTFA Executive was outraged at what seemed to be the administration's repudiation of its agreement, and Fred Wilson, the new UTFA President, persuaded the Council to vote censure of the Provost and of George Connell, the President of the University. At a General Meeting, a majority of UTFA members supported Wilson, though a sizable minority argued that the unprecedented use of a vote of censure against the administration was too harsh a response, and trivialized what should be a weapon of last resort for the Association. Whether properly used or not, the vote of censure does not appear to have had much impact on University policy and, in any event, was withdrawn after a few days. What happened here probably was, that as had happened so often in the past, what UTFA regarded as "negotiations" were regarded by the administration as "discussions," even though the agreement of the Faculty Association was required before any change of policy could be implemented.

For more than a year, there was an impasse on the question of changes in appointments policy. During this time, however, substantial changes were made in the governing structure of the University. Discontent with the operation of the Governing Council and its committees had been increasing as time went on. George Connell was, himself, among the more severe critics of unicameralism. In 1987 the Governing Council was persuaded to sanction a virtual bicameral structure under the umbrella of its own nominal authority. Insofar as academic matters were concerned, this led to the creation of a new "Academic Board" supplanting the old Academic Affairs Committee and, partially, the Planning and Priorities Committee.

Though dominated by academic administrators who are members ex officio, the Academic Board does have a substantial number of elected faculty members. The new body began its work in the fall of 1988, and the Provost turned over to it the question of changes in appointments policy. In due course, the Board created two sub-committees on appointments, one on Policy and Procedures on Academic Appointments, chaired by Cecil Yip, and one on Administrative Appointments, chaired by Paul Perron.

At the beginning, the Faculty Association Executive was optimistic about its dealings with the Academic Board and, in particular, with the Yip Committee. In his Annual Report in the spring of 1990, Fred Wilson wrote of the "good working relationship" between UTFA and Yip's committee, and concluded that "UTFA and the Board are going about the job of re-thinking the Appointments Policy in a truly collegial manner." When, however, the Yip Report was released early in 1991, it became clear such optimism was unjustified. On a number of issues the Yip Report rejected UTFA recommendations and reflected closely the administration's views. In particular the Report's recommendations on appointments for Senior Tutors went directly contrary to UTFA policy.

The question of the rights of tutors has come up repeatedly for many years. Before the Haist Rules were adopted in the 1960s no clear distinction was made between teaching faculty from whom research

158

and publication was expected and faculty whose University duties encompassed teaching only. Tutors, or people who were to become tutors, had, after some years' satisfactory service, permanent appointments on the same basis as tenured faculty members. As the requirements for tenure became more formal in the early 1970s, the tutor category became a kind of catch-all for teaching members of the faculty who were not in a tenure stream, their number amounting eventually to about 9% of total faculty members. Various half-hearted attempts were made over the years to give some regularity to these appointments. Tutors on annual appointments, for example, were distinguished from Senior Tutors of some years' service who served on five-year renewable contracts.

The Faculty Association's intervention in behalf of tutors goes back to the 1970s. Jean Smith, in his first Report on the workings of the Memorandum of Agreement, mentioned, as one of its benefits, the "review of the entire rank structure ... for tutors and senior tutors" undertaken by the Joint Committee. In his first arbitral Report in 1978, Soberman recommended that the progress-through-the-ranks formula be applied to salary settlements for tutors, and the following year after the Provost, Don Chant, had refused to do this, Soberman again awarded tutors a PTR component, but at a lower rate than that for tenured staff. Even that recommendation has never been fully implemented.

In the early 1980s the UTFA Appointments Committee made a number of recommendations concerning tutors which the administration was to ignore. In the spring of 1987 Martin Teplitsky, as part of his mediated settlement, directed the administration and the Faculty Association to set up a Tutors' Committee, with three members from each side, to consider tutors' salary structure and deal with anomalies, including a PTR component still much inferior to that of tenured staff. Once again the administration resisted taking action. When the Yip Committee started work, the Faculty Association strongly recommended that Senior Tutors be given continuing appointments, subject to termination only for cause, as in the case of tenured faculty. What the Yip Report recommended was, not only that five-year contracts be continued, but that Senior Tutors' appointments be terminable specifically either for reasons of "academic planning" or "fiscal exigency," thus making them even more insecure than they had been.

As it happened, the appearance of the Yip Report coincided with the news that two Senior Tutors of many years' satisfactory service, both women incidentally, were to be dismissed for reasons of "academic planning." In response, the UTFA Council agreed not to consider the Yip Report's other recommendations, or negotiate academic appointments policy with the administration until the question of secure appointments for tutors had been satisfactorily resolved.

The Academic Board began its discussions of the Yip Report in the spring of 1991 and finally approved a revised version a year later. The critical moment of the debate on tutors was in January, 1992, and the Board, on almost every issue, followed the lead of the Provost and disregarded the Faculty Association's arguments. Thus, on the Provost's recommendation, Senior Tutors' five-year renewable appointments gave way to continuing appointments but, as these were to be terminable for reasons of academic planning or fiscal exigency, they would provide even less security of tenure than the existing five-year contracts. Those who had hoped the Academic Board would act as a University senate on this matter, independent of the administration, were disappointed. None should have been surprised, given the representative character of the Board. While, for example, out of a membership of 118, there are 20 elected members from the entire Arts and Science faculty, a number of them departmental chairs, there are 22 students and laymen, and about 40 academic administrators serving ex officio or by appointment. It is too soon to make a definitive judgment about the Academic Board, but experience to date

160

suggests that some basic faculty interests at Toronto still must be defended, if at all, by the Faculty Association.

So long as the Memorandum of Agreement remains in place, changes in appointments policies will finally require UTFA agreement. Agreement *can* occasionally be reached with the administration. The Faculty Association, for example, gave general endorsement to the recent recommendations of the Perron Report on policies and procedures in making administrative appointments. In 1991, after years of urging from UTFA, the administration did away with the salary ceilings for associate professors; these had long provided a steady source of grievances. And there has been the substantial redress of inequities in women's appointments and salaries, induced, of course, by legal mandate and governmental and social pressure.

On other equity issues, however, the Faculty Association has made little headway. No arguments have persuaded the administration to re-consider its retirement policy, to index pensions fully, or to address the grievances of tutors. Some equity issues are, of course, intertwined: most tutors are women, for example; and women, who frequently have interrupted careers, suffer even more than men from arbitrary retirement policies and inadequate pensions.

In considering the issues dealt with in very recent years by the Faculty Association, a proper historical reckoning is not possible. This account, therefore, has slipped into a necessarily inconclusive summary of current events, and trembles on the edge of mere prediction. Prediction is, of course, no part of a historian's business, with, perhaps, the single qualification that it is almost always safe to assume that whatever is, will not long stay unchanged. In the spring of 1992 the University is grimly contemplating contraction, not expansion. There is no increase in Provincial funding for the year to come. The University administration's salary offer to the Faculty Association for 1993-94 is zero, less than zero if proposals for a review of the PTR formula are taken seriously. The rate of inflation is the lowest for a generation. These facts of the moment may be, or may not be, portents.

It might be useful, in conclusion, to attempt an estimate of the Faculty Association's achievements and failures over the past half-century, and of its present state and prospects. Its main achievements appear to lie in three areas: first, it has successfully established a decisive faculty role, shared with the University administration, in shaping policies and procedures for making academic appointments, granting tenure, making promotions, and adjudicating grievances. This power, much of which was sketched out in the Haist Rules in the 1960s, has had contractual protection since the Memorandum of Agreement was signed in 1977.

Second, the Faculty Association has achieved significant benefits for Toronto faculty in salary, pensions, and leave policy. The progress-through-the-ranks formula has measurably raised salaries over the past two decades, while the establishment, however briefly, of real collective bargaining with binding arbitration in 1981, produced in the Burkett Award a significant, even if limited, restoration of faculty salary levels.

The third significant achievement of the Faculty Association is less tangible, but important. In moments of crisis, and especially when the University administration has acted wrongly or not at all, the Association has acquired considerable moral weight, and can sometimes speak with authority, not only for the faculty as a whole, but for the University.

On the other hand, the Faculty Association has not been able to secure an adequate faculty role in the top governing structure of the University. It has had only limited success in protecting the weakest and most vulnerable members of the faculty. It has not been able to secure straightforward binding arbitration in salary and benefits disputes. And its powers are defined in a voluntary agreement without any of the legal protection of an agreement reached by a certified union.

There are now about 2,600 faculty members and librarians at the University of Toronto, 28% of whom are women. Their average age is about fifty, compared with an average of forty in the late 1970s. Their average salary in 1992-93 will be about $85,000, which, largely as a function of age, represents a rough restoration of the pre-war relationship of University salaries to those in other professions. Just over two-thirds (67.5%) of these people are members of the Faculty Association (which also has some 300 retired members). This proportion has remained stable for a generation, except for falling in the early 1970s and rising in 1977.

A number of constituencies have more than 80% of their potential membership—Library Science and Librarians, the Faculty of Education, St. Michael's, Victoria, New and Innis Colleges, the Humanities division at Scarborough College, the Sociology Department, and several language departments. A number of constituencies, however, have fewer than half their potential members—Economics, Computer Science and Statistics, Management Studies, Mechanical Engineering, and several departments in the Faculty of Medicine and other Health Sciences. Within Arts and Science there have been some changes in patterns of membership in recent years. Membership has increased, for example, in Botany and Zoology where it had been low, and fallen in History, English, and Philosophy where it had been high.

The physical resources of the Faculty Association have grown significantly in comparison with those of earlier times. After seventeen years in cramped and shabby offices in the Tip Top Building, the Association moved, in 1987, into blandly corporate quarters only a few blocks north on Spadina Avenue, but well away from the squalor, colour and bustle of its old neighbourhood. There is a permanent staff of four, including, now, two lawyers. Replacing the single typewriter and dented filing cabinet of the 1960s is a considerable little array of office equipment—two photo-copy machines, seven computers, a laser printer and a fax machine. Association income and expenditures are now over a million dollars annually, and current reserves are around $700,000.

The UTFA President from 1990 to 1992 has been Bonnie Horne, the first woman as well as the first professional librarian to hold the office. Both she and Fred Wilson, who served as President from 1987 to 1990, had considerable earlier experience on the Executive. Several members of the current Executive have served for some years, and the incoming President, Bill Graham, is completing three years as president of OCUFA. There is occasional complaint among some Council members at the continuity of the Executive, but there is also obvious justification for it as a function of the increased professionalization of the Association.

While the Council is, on the whole, better-attended than in earlier times, and many UTFA members serve faithfully on standing committees, participation in Association activities by members-at-large may well be less frequent than formerly. Certainly attendance at general meetings is poor. Neither the Annual General Meeting of 1988 nor that of 1989 had the required quorum of 100 members present, nor did a second attempt at an Annual Meeting in 1988. The Annual Meetings in 1990 and 1991 were held, but the 1992 Annual Meeting again lacked a quorum. It is true that there have been a few well-attended Special Meetings in recent years, reflecting faculty anger, apprehension, or concern about some issue or another, and the conventional wisdom of people active in the Association holds that inattendance at meetings reflects the members' quiet approval. It may also partly reflect the reluctance of Toronto faculty, noticeable at least since 1970, to take part voluntarily in any communal activities at the University.

Inevitably active members of the Association have come and gone over the years, retiring, leaving the University, or simply doing other things. A number have been drawn into University administration: Art Kruger and Frank Iacobucci in the 1970s; more recently, Carole Moore, who became Chief Librarian of the University, Paul Thompson, who became Principal of Scarborough College, and, most notably, Michael Finlayson who, in 1991, became the University's Vice-President, Human Resources, charged with, among other duties, negotiating salary and benefits with the Faculty Association.[*]

A few active members have resigned from the Association, finding themselves out of sympathy with one or another of its policies: Keith Yates, David Huntley, Nanda Choudhry, and Jean Smith come to mind, though Smith has recently re-joined. Others have followed Stan Schiff's example, retaining UTFA membership but distancing themselves from its activities.

If, however, the Faculty Association has, in general, kept the support of the faculty, now for half a century, it is presumably because it serves a function, or functions, members see as useful. In one way, obviously, it is like any trade union, seeking to gain and maintain benefits for its members. The faculty, however, has never regarded such benefits as merely economic. They have always included the perceived essentials for professional well-being, and these, given the nature of a university, are somewhat open-ended. Academic freedom must be a central concern of organized faculty members at any vital university. And, in order to mean anything, academic freedom must be broadly enough defined to encompass, not merely the individual needs of professors, but the climate in which they work. Thus the Faculty Association at Toronto has properly taken an interest in such matters as the governance of the University, treatment of University

---

[*] After this was written, Adel Sedra, early in 1993, accepted appointment as Vice-President and Provost of the University.

employees other than faculty, policies towards students, and a range of general administrative practices throughout the University.

This breadth of concern, however, brings the Faculty Association necessarily into conflict with the University administration on a wider front than is usual in the relations between workers and management. Most University administrators are themselves faculty members who see their own duties as more than managerial. They too see *themselves* as guardians of the University, its freedoms and immunities. There does not appear to be any simple way to resolve this conflict of perceptions. Perhaps it should merely be accepted. It certainly serves little purpose for the Faculty Association and the University administration, each to question the legitimacy of the other. They are colleagues and they are adversaries. So it has been, and so, presumably, it will be.

Appendix

Faculty Association Chairmen and Presidents, 1947-1992

Chairmen of the CRTS (Committee to Represent the Teaching Staff) until 1954, and of the ATS (Association of the Teaching Staff) from 1954 to 1971 were elected at the Fall Meeting and served for a year beginning in late November or early December. Since the establishment of UTFA (University of Toronto Faculty Association) in 1971, presidents have begun their terms on July 1. Service of CRTS and ATS chairmen was sometimes casual, and on three occasions, in the absence of the elected chairman, others chaired the Spring Meeting and led the association for some time following it. These acting chairmen were F.E.W. Wetmore (Chemistry) in 1954, B. Laskin (Law) in 1961, and J.B. Conacher (History) in 1965. All UTFA presidents have been acclaimed except for H.L. Dyck, who defeated A.S. Sedra (Electrical Engineering) in 1981, and F.F. Wilson, who defeated H.E. Rogers (Linguistics) in 1987.

Chairmen, Committee to Represent the Teaching Staff:

1947-48	V.W. Bladen (Political Economy)
1948-49	G.B. Langford (Geology)
1949-50	G.deB. Robinson (Mathematics)
1950-52	J.T. Wilson (Geophysics)
1952-54	W.G. Raymore (Architecture)

Chairmen, Association of the Teaching Staff:

1954-57	K.C. Fisher (Zoology)
1957-59	C.R. Myers (Psychology)
1959-61	R.M. Saunders (History)
1961-62	K.S. Bernhardt (Psychology)
1962-64	B. Laskin (Law)
1964-65	C.B. Macpherson (Political Economy)
1965-67	G.F.D. Duff (Mathematics)
1967-68	M.F. Grapko (Child Study)
1968-69	F.E. Winter (Fine Arts)
1969-70	J.M. Rist (Classics)
1970-71	R.W. Missen (Chemical Engineering)

Presidents, University of Toronto Faculty Association:

1971-72	J.B. Conacher (History)
1972-73	S.M. Uzumeri (Civil Engineering)
1973-76	W.H. Nelson (History)
1976-77	J.M. Daniels (Physics)
1977-79	J.E. Smith (Political Science)
1979-81	M.G. Finlayson (History)
1981-83	H.L. Dyck (History)
1983-84	C.C. Yip (Banting & Best)
1984-85	J.P Dyson (English)
1985-87	M.G. Finlayson (History)
1987-90	F.F. Wilson (Philosophy)
1990-92	B.L. Horne (Library)
1992-	W.C. Graham (Philosophy)

Index

Index

Donnelly, Michael W., 138, 141, 146
Dues, 8, 16, 64, 101, 114, 115, 147, 148, 149, 164
Duff-Berdahl Report, 34-35
Duff, George F. D., 17
Duff, Sir James, 34
Dupré, J. Steven, 47
Dyck, Harvey L., 105, 116-117, 123-134, 135, 137, 138, 139, 140-141, 145-146, 148
Dyson, J. Peter, 139-142, 143-146

Eayrs, James G., 31
Eberts, Mary A., 106, 107
Economics, Department of, 98, 130, 163
Education, Faculty of, 163
Elite, Sue Ann, 143
Engineering, Faculty of Applied Science and, 68, 70, 78, 98, 99-100, 105, 113, 123, 124-125, 128, 163
English, Department of, 83, 90-91, 106, 139, 163
Equity issues, 20, 73, 139, 151-161
Estes, James M., 140, 146
Etkin, Bernard, 68
Evans, John R., 77-78, 82-83, 84, 87-89, 91, 94, 95, 108, 111, 112, 124, 136, 141

Faculty Reform Caucus, 72-73, 78, 105
Finlayson, Michael G., 71, 79-81, 86, 89, 93, 94, 120, 121, 122-123, 127, 131, 145-149, 155-156, 165

Fisher, Kenneth C., 18, 27
Fitting, Peter, 105, 142, 146
Foley, Joan E., 157, 160
Forster, Donald F., 84, 91, 94, 136
Fowke, Vernon C., 28-29
Friedland, Martin L., 49
Frye, H. Northrop, 91

GAA (Graduate Assistants' Association), 105, 106, 126, 131
Gauthier, David P., 105
Geology, Department of, 18
Gordon, Walter, 10
Governing Act of 1971, 51-55, 72, 131
Governing Council, 46, 51, 52-55, 73, 76, 77, 80, 86, 107, 108, 110, 119, 121-122, 127, 128, 131, 133, 135-139, 141, 142, 143, 158
Grabb, Victoria, 127-128, 131, 140, 143-144, 145, 151
Graham, William C., 149, 164
Grapko, Michael F., 38
Graydon, William M., 128, 130
Greene, Robert A., 50, 69-70
Grievances, faculty, 89-91, 106, 107-108, 109, 110, 119, 137, 139, 144, 151-152, 154-155, 161, 162
Guelph, University of, 136

Haist Rules, 33, 56, 106, 109, 158, 162
Haist, Reginald E., 33
Hallett, Archibald C. H., 90, 106
Ham, James M., 50, 124-125, 128, 129, 131, 136

171

172